The widely acclaimed
University of Chicago

C[...]

David Grene and Richmond Lattimore

A complete collection of the tragedies of Aeschylus, Sophocles, and Euripides rendered in modern translations reflecting a rare fidelity to the spirit, the rhythm, and the meaning of the original texts.

TITLES IN PRINT

FORTHCOMING TITLES

The Complete Greek Tragedies
Edited by David Grene and Richmond Lattimore

Aeschylus I

Oresteia:
Agamemnon
The Libation Bearers
The Eumenides

Translated and with an
Introduction by Richmond Lattimore

WSP
Ⓗ WASHINGTON SQUARE PRESS, INC. • NEW YORK

The Complete Greek Tragedies

AESCHYLUS I

University of Chicago Press edition published May, 1953

A *Washington Square Press* edition
1st printing..........................May, 1967

Published by
Washington Square Press, Inc., 630 Fifth Avenue, New York, N.Y.

WASHINGTON SQUARE PRESS editions are distributed in the
U.S. by Simon & Schuster, Inc., 630 Fifth Avenue, New
York, N.Y. 10020 and in Canada by Simon & Schuster
of Canada, Ltd., Richmond Hill, Ontario, Canada.

CONTENTS

NOTE

The translation of *Agamemnon* which is here used first appeared in *Greek Plays in Modern Translation,* edited with an Introduction by Dudley Fitts (New York: Dial Press, 1947). It is used here by kind permission of The Dial Press, Inc. Some alterations have been made, chiefly in the matter of spelling Greek names. Two sections of *Agamemnon,* "The God of War, Money Changer of Dead Bodies," and "The Achaeans Have Got Troy, upon This Very Day," first published in *War and the Poet: A Comprehensive Anthology of the World's Great War Poetry,* edited by Richard Eberhart and Selden Rodman, are used by permission of the Devin-Adair Company.

The translation of all three plays is based on H. W. Smyth's "Loeb Classical Library" text (London and New York: William Heinemann, Ltd., and G. P. Putnam's Sons 1926). A few deviations from this text occur where I have followed the manuscript readings instead of emendations accepted by Smyth.

Various editions of Greek drama divide the lines of lyric passages in various ways, but editors regularly follow the traditional line numbers whether their own line divisions tally with these numbers or not. This accounts for what may appear to be erratic line numbering in our translations, for instance, *The Eumenides* 360 and following. The line numbering in the translations in this volume is that of Smyth's text.

INTRODUCTION TO
THE *ORESTEIA*

The Life of Aeschylus

AESCHYLUS, the son of Euphorion, was born in the last
quarter of the sixth century B.C., probably about 513 or 512
B.C. The great Persian Wars occurred during his early manhood, and he fought, certainly at Marathon (where his
brother was killed in action) and probably also at Artemi-
sium, Salamis, and Plataea. He is said to have begun at an
early age to write tragedies; his first victory was in 484 B.C.
In or about 476 B.C. he visited Sicily and, at the instance of
Hieron of Syracuse, Pindar's friend, produced *The Women
of Etna* at the new city of Etna which Hieron had founded.
In 472 he produced his *Persians* at Athens, with Pericles as
his choregus (or official sponsor) and re-produced it, pre-
sumably in the next year, in Sicily. Back in Athens in 468,
he was defeated by the young Sophocles, but won again in
467 with a set of plays including *The Seven against Thebes*.
In 458 he presented the *Oresteia* (*Agamemnon*, *The Libation
Bearers*, *The Eumenides*). He died in Gela, Sicily, in 456 or
455 B.C., leaving behind him an epitaph which might be
rendered as follows:

Under this monument lies Aeschylus the Athenian,
   Euphorion's son, who died in the wheatlands of Gela.
    The grove
 of Marathon with its glories can speak of his valor in
    battle.

I

The long-haired Persian remembers and can speak
of it too.

He left behind more than seventy plays (the exact number
is uncertain), of which seven have survived. They are *The
Suppliants, The Persians, The Seven against Thebes, Prometheus Bound, Agamemnon, The Libation Bearers, The
Eumenides*. He is said to have won first prize thirteen times
while he lived, but after his death his tragedies were often
produced again, and in competition with living poets he won
more prizes still.

It would be interesting to know how old Aeschylus was
when he wrote his known and dated plays. But the date of
his birth is quite uncertain, though the year 525/4[1] is com-
monly given as if it were an established fact. It is true
enough that apparently independent authorities give ages at
the time of Marathon and at time of death which agree with
this scheme. However, the birth date may very easily be
accounted for by the rule-of-thumb method, favored by
Greek chronologists, of taking an important event in a man's
life and counting back forty years to an estimated date of
birth. Thus the traditional birth date of Thucydides is 471
(from the outbreak of the war he recorded in 431); of
Aristophanes, 445 (from the production of his masterpiece,
The Frogs, in 405). Both these dates are bad (there are
many parallels), and the one for Aeschylus is no more con-
vincing. An age of forty at his first victory is suspect, not
only because it tallies so neatly with a known method of
reckoning, but because it is in itself unlikely that a man who
utterly eclipsed his rivals in subsequent reputation, so that
they are now very little more than bare names, should have
had to wait so long before scoring his first success. A less

[1] Athenian dates are generally fixed by the term of the *archon,* or
titular chief magistrate. Since the archons changed over some time in
the summer, not at our new year, such dates overlap those of our
calendar. Since, however, plays came out in the spring before the
change-over, a play dated to an archonship of, for instance, 485/4 will
always fall in 484.

popular but more attractive tradition would make him born in 513 or 512, but here also we may be dealing with estimates based on known and dated events, such as battles and dramatic productions.

Ancient authorities also tell us a few other things about Aeschylus which would be interesting if we could believe them. It is said that he left Athens for Sicily in chagrin because he was defeated by Simonides, the great lyric poet, in a competition for writing the epitaph of the dead at Marathon, or because he was defeated by Sophocles in dramatic competition, or because he disliked Athenian politics.[2] The defeats are real, but they do not tally, chronologically, with the visits to Sicily; on the contrary, after losing to Sophocles, Aeschylus stayed in Athens and won first prize with *The Seven against Thebes* and its related dramas the next year, which is quite different from going off to Sicily in a huff. If one may guess at why he went to Sicily, it was because Sicily was the America of that day, the new Greek world, rich, generous, and young, with its own artists but without the tradition of perfected culture which Old Greece had built up, and it attracted Pindar, Bacchylides, Simonides, and Aeschylus much as America has attracted English men of letters from Dickens, Thackeray, and Wilde down to the present day. We do not know much about the personal character of Aeschylus and can make little critical use of what we do know. The epitaph shows he was proud of his military record, but this scarcely helps us to understand *The Persians, The Seven against Thebes,* or *Agamemnon.* We must approach Aeschylus, not from the biographies, but from his own plays.

---

[2] Euripides, near the end of his life, left Athens in voluntary exile and died in Macedonia at the court of King Archelaus. There is reason to believe that he left because he had constantly failed to win critical approval in Athens and because he despaired of the hopeless course which his city had been following since the time of Pericles. The biographers doubtless applied the analogy of Euripides-Athens-Archelaus to Aeschylus-Athens-Hieron. But Euripides was a failure in his own lifetime, and it made him a defeatist and escapist. Of Aeschylus we can say with confidence that he was neither of these things.

Early Tragedy

From the time of the almost legendary Thespis, a full generation before the earliest tragedy we possess, dramatic performances of some sort had been regularly produced at Athens. In origin, they must have been a special local development of the choral lyric—sacred, occasional, provincial, public—which was alive in all the cities of Greece. But the early phases of the course by which dramatic lyric was transformed into lyric drama are now invisible to us. We can recognize certain ingredients, or essential features. Early drama was choral, and the life of Attic tragedy shows the indispensable chorus to the end, though the actors steadily invade the preserves of the chorus until, at the close of the fifth century, Euripides is using it sometimes in a most perfunctory manner, as if it were a convention he could not get rid of but might otherwise have preferred to do without. Early drama was sacred, having to do with the cult of divinities, and particularly with the cult of Dionysus: on the formal side, it was performed to the end on ground devoted to that god and before his priest; but developed tragedy did not have to be *about* Dionysus, and seldom was. Like most choral lyric, it was given through the medium of a formal competition. The early tragic poets drew, for narrative material and for metrical forms, on an already rich and highly developed tradition of nondramatic poetry, epic and lyric. They also drew, no doubt, on the unwritten and almost inarticulate experience of a living people, on folk memory and folklore, cult and ritual and ceremony and passion play and mystery play. But tragedy did not grow out of such elements. It was made. Concerning the makers, we know little indeed about Thespis, Pratinas, Choerilus, Phrynichus. Tragedy, for us, begins with Aeschylus.

By or during the career of Aeschylus, the features of Greek tragedy become fixed. At an Athenian festival, three player-groups, each consisting of two (later three) actors

4

and chorus, act out competitively four-drama sets. The material is based on stories told or indicated in previous Greek legend. Tragedy is heroic. The costumes are formal, physical action restrained and without violence; naturalism is neither achieved nor desired. Aeschylus himself, and his older contemporary Phrynichus before him, experimented with dramatic stories taken from contemporary history, and of these we have *The Persians*, dealing with the repulse of Xerxes and his forces. This was a success, but circumstances in this case were favorable to special occasional drama, for the defeat of Persia was the proudest achievement of Greek history. And, even here, the play is *about* the Persians, not the Greeks, the setting is Persia, and only Persian individuals are named. Remoteness from the immediate here-and-now, required by tragedy and guaranteed by legendary material, is here to a great extent achieved by placing the scene in the heart of Persia, so far away and guarded from Greeks that to the audience it might have seemed almost as legendary as the Troy of Hector or the Thebes of Oedipus.[3] A drama dealing directly with Themistocles and Pericles or with the war between Athens and Aegina would have been neither desired by the poet nor tolerated by his audience.

The body of legend on which Aeschylus and the other tragic poets drew was composed of the epic poems of Homer and his successors and constituted a loose and informal, but fairly comprehensive, history of the world as the Greeks knew it. Typical sources in this complex were the *Iliad* and the *Odyssey;* the "Epic Cycle," or series of subsequent epics which filled out the story of Troy and dealt in detail with its occasions and aftereffects; the epics that told the story of Thebes; and numerous other narratives either written down or transmitted through unwritten oral tradition. The dramatist rarely worked directly from the main body of the *Iliad*

[3] So Shakespeare drew on history and legend for his tragedies and romances, or, when these dealt with time not specifically antique, the place would be idealized by distance and the vagueness of his audience's information: Italy, Bohemia, Illyria, Arden.

or the *Odyssey;* the less authoritative minor texts were more popular. The dramatist seems not to have felt free to invent his material outright, but he could—in fact, he must— choose among variants, expand or deepen and interpret character, generally shape the story on the trend of his own imagination. In the case of Aeschylus, this process can be best reconstructed in the *Oresteia,* the trilogy or sequence of three tragedies composed of *Agamemnon, The Libation Bearers,* and *The Eumenides.*

The Story of the House of Atreus

The version of the legend as Aeschylus used it runs as follows. Atreus and Thyestes, the sons of Pelops, quarreled because Thyestes had seduced his brother's wife, and disputed the throne of Argos. Thyestes, defeated and driven out, returned as a suppliant with his children, and Atreus in pretended reconciliation invited him and his children to a feast. There he slaughtered the children of Thyestes (all but one) and served them in a concealing dish to their father, who ate their flesh. When it was made known to him what he had been doing, Thyestes cursed the entire house and fled with his surviving son, Aegisthus. Agamemnon and Menelaus, the sons of Atreus, inherited the Kingdom of Argos, and married, respectively, Clytaemestra and Helen, the daughters of Tyndareus the Spartan. Clytaemestra bore Agamemnon three children—Iphigeneia, Electra, and Orestes. When Paris of Troy seduced Helen and carried her away, the brothers organized a great expedition to win her back. The armament, gathered at Aulis, was held there by wind and weather; Calchas the prophet divined that this was due to the anger of Artemis and, with the pressure of public opinion behind him, forced Agamemnon to sacrifice his daughter Iphigeneia, in order to appease the goddess. Agamemnon with his forces sailed to Troy and in the tenth year captured it, destroyed the city and its temples, killed or enslaved the people, and set sail for home. On the sea, a great storm struck the fleet, and Agamemnon, with a single galley, made his way back to Argos, the rest of his ships being sunk or driven out of sight and knowledge. With him he brought his mistress, Cassandra, captive princess and prophetess of Troy.

Meanwhile, in Argos, Aegisthus had returned and Clytaemestra had taken him as her lover and sent Orestes out of the country. Warned of the king's approach by signal flares through which he had agreed to notify her of the fall of Troy, she made ready to receive him. She welcomed him into the house, but when he was unarmed in his bath, she pinioned him in a robe and stabbed him to death, and killed Cassandra as well. She defended her action before the people of Argos, who were helpless against Aegisthus and his bodyguard. But Orestes returned at last and was welcomed by his sister Electra, who had remained rebellious against her mother but without power to act. Orestes, disguised as a traveler and pretending to bring news of his own death, won access to the house and killed both Aegisthus and Clytaemestra. Portents and dreams had forewarned of this murder, and Orestes had been encouraged, even commanded, by Apollo to carry it through. Nevertheless, when he had displayed the bodies and defended his act, the Furies (Eumenides), or spirits of retribution, appeared to him and drove him out of Argos. Orestes took refuge with Apollo at Delphi and was at last purified of the murder, but the Furies refused to acknowledge any absolution and pursued him across the world until he took refuge on the rock of Athens before the statue of Athene. There, in the presence of Athene, Apollo and the Furies appealed to her for a decision, and she, thinking the case too difficult to be judged by a single person, even her divine self, appointed a court of Athenian jurors to hear the arguments and judge the case. When the votes of these resulted in a tie, Athene herself cast the deciding ballot in favor of Orestes. Orestes, deeply grateful to Athene and her city, returned to Argos, while Athene found it necessary to propitiate the angry Eumenides by inducing them to accept an honorable place as tutelary spirits in Athens. The law court of the Areiopagus, which had judged the case, was perpetuated as a just tribunal for homicide down through the history of man.

Variations of the Legend

Such are the bare facts of the story, the raw stuff out of which Aeschylus forged three massive tragedies. The story of the murder of Agamemnon had been told by Homer in the *Odyssey*[4] and by the cyclic successors of Homer in the *Nostoi* ("Returns"), while the early part of the story appears in the *Cypria*. Stesichorus, the Sicilian poet, had made the fortunes of Orestes the subject of a long narrative in lyric form; and Pindar in his *Eleventh Pythian* had summarized the tale and reflected on the motives of Clytaemestra; and others, too, had touched on the story. On all these Aeschylus doubtless drew, and he had numerous variations from which to pick and choose.[5] The main difference between Aeschylus and Homer is to be found, however, not in details but in the whole approach to the story, which, in turn, motivates selection, addition, or omission of detail. It is to be noted that Homer does not tell the story consecutively; he really does not tell it at all, but he draws on it for example and illustration. The homecoming of Agamemnon is played against the homecoming of Odysseus; the situations are analogous, but the characters are different and bring different results

---

4 Piecemeal: the plot is constantly referred to by analogy with the plot of the *Odyssey*. The principal references are: i. 29–43, Zeus calls the vengeance of Orestes an example of just retribution; i. 298–300, Athene uses it as an encouragement to Telemachus; iii. 254–312, Nestor tells Telemachus of the beguiling of Clytaemestra, the wanderings of Menelaus, and the vengeance of Orestes; iv. 514–37, Menelaus tells how he heard from Proteus about the death of Agamemnon; xi. 405–34, the ghost of Agamemnon tells Odysseus how his wife and Aegisthus murdered him and Cassandra.

5 For example, Homer makes the scene of the murder (and consequently the palace of Agamemnon) Mycenae; Stesichorus and Simonides, Sparta; Pindar, Amyclae (which comes to the same thing); Aeschylus, Argos, doubtless for political reasons. Stesichorus called the nurse of Orestes Laodameia; Pindar, Arsinoë; Aeschylus, Cilissa; etc.

out of similar materials. The murderous suitors lurk in the house of Odysseus as did Aegisthus in that of Agamemnon, but Penelope has not joined the enemy as Clytaemestra did. Nevertheless, when Odysseus comes home, he has his warning from the ghost of Agamemnon and goes warily so as not to fall into a similar trap. As for Telemachus, the resolute activity of Orestes is set as an example against his own indecision. The parts of the story that bear on such an apposition come out, and the tendency of it varies accordingly. The story is a domestic tragedy, but, since the house is a king's house, the tragedy becomes dynastic also. It begins with the betrayal of a king and the alienation of his kingdom and ends with the rewinning of dynastic power by the rightful heir. Therefore, though the death of Agamemnon is tragic, the deaths of Aegisthus and Clytaemestra are nothing of the sort; no tragedy adheres to Orestes, he merits no compassion, only praise. It is, I think, because of this *approach* that Homer fails to mention certain aspects of the story which are prominent in Attic tragedy. Iphigeneia does not appear; her slaughter would have suggested some motive of justice mixed into the treachery of Clytaemestra. Nor do we hear of the wrongs inflicted by Atreus on Thyestes and his sons, for this would have made the murder of Agamemnon in some measure defensible as an act of retribution. Nowhere in Homer do we hear of an Orestes pursued by the Furies of his mother, whether these might be actual spirits or the remorse in his own memory. Did Homer, then, know nothing of how Orestes murdered Clytaemestra? The lines in which he speaks of her death betray him (*Od.* iii. 304–10), for, while Menelaus was still on his travels,

Seven years Aegisthus was lord in golden Mycenae,
but in the eighth the evil came on him when great Orestes
came back from Athens and killed his father's slayer, the crafty
Aegisthus, who had murdered his glorious father. And after

he had killed him, in the Argives' presence he held a
funeral
for his mother, who was hateful, and for the coward
Aegisthus.

This unobtrusive notice is all we have, but it makes perfectly
plain the fact that the matricide was in Homer's tradition,
and he could not contradict it. But he was in a position to
place the emphasis wherever he chose and to tell only as
much of the story, or as little, as suited his purpose. It is
surely no accident that the parts which he leaves out are
those which would complicate and confuse his simple picture of Aegisthus as a conspiring villain, Orestes as an
avenging hero, and Clytaemestra as a woman who yielded to
her weakness.

Aeschylus, on the other hand, told the whole story. *Agamemnon* takes us from the news of Troy's fall to the murder
of Agamemnon and the confirmation of his murderers as
despots in Argos. *The Libation Bearers* begins with the return of Orestes and ends with his flight from Argos, pursued
by the Furies, after the murder of Clytaemestra and Aegisthus. *The Eumenides* finds Orestes seeking sanctuary at
Delphi, takes him to Athens for his acquittal and absolution,
and ends with the establishment of the Furies in their new
home at Athens. Further, particularly in the first play of the
trilogy, there are constant cutbacks which sweep into the
drama much of the foregoing material: the banquet of
Thyestes, the sacrifice of Iphigeneia, the siege and fall of
Troy. The simple narrative which we can reconstruct from
notices in Homer could not have carried the weight of a
tragic trilogy.

"Agamemnon"

Agamemnon is, first of all, a domestic tragedy. The dominant figure, Clytaemestra, is a wife estranged through the
wrong her husband committed on their daughter; love for

Iphigeneia, acting through the murder of Agamemnon, is on its way toward driving her to fight her love for her surviving daughter and for her son. Her paramour and partner is her husband's cousin. Behind them all is the figure of Helen, Clytaemestra's sister, wife of Agamemnon's brother, whose treachery caused the Trojan War, Iphigeneia's death, and all the estrangement and broken faith that followed. The theme here is the *philos-aphilos* or hate-in-love; its drive is the dynamic force of contradiction.

Behind the domestic tragedy lies the tragedy of war. For the sake of Helen, whose beauty was unforgettable but whose worth could not be demonstrated by reason or defended by argument, Agamemnon drained Greece of its manhood and involved the innocent in the miseries of a bitter campaign. The Trojans welcomed Helen and her captor and so were guilty; but their punishment—the total destruction of their city, their temples, and their men; the enslavement and defiling of their women and children—was out of all proportion to any harm they had done to Greece. Neither Troy nor Greece deserved what the idea of Helen made Agamemnon do to them. For he destroyed his own country as well as Troy; many died in the years before Ilium; the survivors were drowned or scattered in the great storm on the way back; and the pomp of his entrance thinly disguises the fact that he brought home the crew of a single ship.

Because of this, with the war tragedy goes political tragedy as well. The means by which this is communicated is through the chorus, who, in so far as they function as characters in the play, represent the solid elders of Argos. These are king's men, since the king in the heroic period stands for lawful authority; they have seen that Agamemnon's expedition was wrong, and they tell him so (799–804), but they would still be loyal to him if he were a much worse man than he is. It is these sturdy citizens who tell how, as the death reports and the urns full of ashes came in from the front, the people at home began to mutter against the king and ask why the war was fought; and, though the chorus cannot take their part, they cannot deny that there is cause for such mutterings. But the people did find a champion, or so they thought, at least a leader, Aegisthus, the king's cousin. He took advantage of the disaffection among those who hated the king he hated, and so returned from exile; he won the throne by winning the queen, confirmed his seizure by contriving the murder of Agamemnon, and defended it with his tyrant's personal bodyguard.[6]

Thus we come about once more to the dynastic tragedy of Homer. But the interpretations of Agamemnon's murder do not exclude one another. Aeschylus can work on several levels at once. The war tragedy and the political tragedy do not contradict, they cohere with and deepen the tragedy of persons.

On the personal level, *Agamemnon* works through a com-

---

[6] The word *tyrannos* ("tyrant") was used by the Greek prose writers in a semi-technical sense, and it only gradually became a term of reproach. The tyrant was a self-appointed despot whose career was characteristic in various places at various times in Greek history, but especially in the seventh and sixth centuries B.C. The Athenian using the word would think at once of his own tyrants, Peisistratus and his son Hippias; the restoration of the latter was still a political issue when Aeschylus was a young man. The following may serve as a general description of the typical early tyrant. He was an aristocrat, but one who was likely not to be in power while the government remained stable. He posed as a representative of the underprivileged and won and used their support, but generally got his position by unconstitutional means. His policy was generally to hold more than royal power without assuming any formal title, through influence and threat. He nevertheless always attempted to found a permanent dynasty through his sons, but hardly ever succeeded. His championship of the poorer classes was generally more than a pose, and he frequently worked toward broadening the base of democracy. Thus his most persistent enemies were not the masses but his fellow-aristocrats, except for the few he could win over into his own personal following; but, because, in spite of all the good he might do, his very existence flouted all legality, those who loved law and liberty hated him too. He had to guard himself, and infallible signs of his presence were the bodyguard of professionals and the spy system. Tyranny was one of the great growing pains in the life of young democracy, and history has been unkind to the tyrant, but for solid reasons.

Tyranny actually came later than Homeric or heroic kingship, and Aeschylus probably knew very well that it was anachronistic to see in

plex of collisions, not so much right against wrong as right
against right, each person insisting on his right with the
force of passion. Agamemnon, the king, with a king's power
and pride in arms, appears briefly and is relatively simple.
Pride would have driven him without hesitation to undertake
the recovery of Helen, and this decision sets in motion a
chain of events which becomes increasingly inescapable. The
sacrifice of Iphigeneia, the persistence in besieging Troy,
even the intrigue with Cassandra, follow necessarily; his
pride grows on its own acts, until just before death he is a
swollen vanity. He himself began the series of acts which
pile up to overwhelm him, but, looking back, one cannot see
where a proud king could have chosen otherwise. Clytaemestra's motives are far more complex. Homer had made
her act in simple surrender and consequent betrayal. But
Pindar speculated on motives which would, if admitted by
Homer, have spoiled the cast of his version:

> Was it Iphigeneia, who at the Euripos crossing
> was slaughtered far from home,
> that vexed her to drive in anger the hand of violence?
> Or was it couching in a strange bed

Aegisthus' usurpation a tyrant's *coup de main*. Yet he seems to have
committed that anachronism. When the chorus hear Agamemnon's
death cries and sense murder by the queen and her lover, one of them
says (1354-55; see also 1365): "Anyone can see it, by these first steps
they have taken, they purpose to be tyrants here upon our city." In
speaking of tyranny (*tyrannis*) here, either Aeschylus is using the
word strictly, or he is not. He might use "tyrant" loosely, as a syn-
onym for *basileus*, "king" (Euripides does this). But then the statement would have no point whatever, for what could the chorus expect
other than that the murderer would make himself king? Plainly, they
fear life not only under the wrong ruler but under the wrong kind of
government. Historically, the tyrant overthrew a republic (the lawful
constitution), but, in the heroic age on which tragedy drew, there was
no republic; the lawful constitution was kingship; therefore, the tyrant
overthrew this. When Aegisthus at last appears, he has his tyrant's
bodyguard. It is impossible not to connect Aegisthus' *coup de main*
with the rebellious murmuring of the masses against the king and his
war. But the political pattern is a submotif, not fully worked out; its
main effect is to shadow the character of Aegisthus—seducer, murderer, usurper already—with the dark memory of the hated historical
tyrant.

by night that broke her will and sent her awry—for
young wives
a sin most vile.[7]

Two motives to choose from: Iphigeneia or Aegisthus. But
Pindar has already mentioned Cassandra and so implied a
third alternative, mother-resentment, guilty love, or jealousy.
After Pindar, we could choose A or B or C. Aeschylus ignores
the "or" and takes them all. Clytaemestra has loved Agamemnon, Iphigeneia has made her hate him, she loves
Aegisthus. But her love for Agamemnon was real, and
enough of that love remains to waken perfectly real jealousy
at the sight of Agamemnon's lovely captive. This also moves
her enormous pride, which amounts to unprecedented ambition for dynastic power. The women of the heroic age are
represented as people of character, with will and temper of
their own; but if their men insist, they must give way. Force
them and they love. Cassandra, Clytaemestra's foil and rival,
has seen her city and people wiped out by Agamemnon, her
father and brothers butchered by his followers, but she
clings to him. So Briseis in the *Iliad* clings to Achilles, who
has personally killed her husband, and so Sophocles makes
his Tecmessa protest to Aias that she loves him, for she has
no one else, since he has destroyed her home.[8] Not so
Clytaemestra, who, like Helen her sister, chooses her own
loves. Again, the code obviously allowed the warlord, married
or unmarried, to have the comforts of a captive mistress on
campaign. But if Clytaemestra did not like a code, she would
smash it. With her "male strength of heart in its high
confidence," she steps boldly from the sphere of women's
action into that of men;[9] like a king, she handles the city in

---

[7] Pindar *Pyth.* 11. 22–25, trans. Lattimore.

[8] The most detailed Attic study of the womanly woman in the heroic
age is Euripides' *Andromache* in the play named after her. It is she
who says (213–14): "A wife, even if she is given to a worthless man,
should cling to him, not set her will up against his." It is noteworthy
that her definitions of a woman's duties occur in debate with her
Spartan rival, Hermione, daughter of Menelaus and Helen.

[9] When she refers to herself as "a mere woman," it is with massive
sarcasm (348, 590–97, 1661).

her lord's absence, and to her the hostile and suspicious chorus turns with unwilling admiration. When the chorus doubts her intelligences, again when after the murder they openly challenge her, she faces them down and silences them; and it is only on the appearance of Aegisthus, whom they despise as they cannot despise Clytaemestra, that they break out rebelliously again. Even in deceit, as in shameless defiance, she is stately (855–88, 1667). She is the born aristocrat, heiress by birth as by marriage to the power and wealth of kings, and so contemptuous of the *nouveau riche* (1042–46). Everything she does and says is in the grand manner. The chain of beacon fires linking Argos and Troy, defeating distance and time, is a characteristically grand gesture, and worthy of it are the arrogant lines in which she concludes her story of relayed signal flares (315–16):

> By such proof and such symbol I announce to you
> my lord at Troy has sent his messengers to me.

Such is the spirit of her grandiose welcome to Agamemnon, the purple carpet on which he is forced to walk to his butchery, and the words in which such lavish outlay is defended, "the sea is there," with its plain implication that "the sea is ours."

Such characteristics give Clytaemestra stature, but in no sense justify her. It is not only that, in asserting her right, or at least determination, to act as freely as a man, she has taken to her bed the "womanish" Aegisthus. The whole house has been wrong since the quarrel of Atreus and Thyestes. Atreus was hideous in murder, but this does not justify Aegisthus in murdering Agamemnon, any more than the sins of Agamemnon justified his murder by Clytaemestra, or the sins of Paris and Helen justified the obliteration of Troy. All the executioners plead that they act for just retribution, but the chain of murder has got out of hand and is perpetuating itself, until it seems no longer to come from personal purpose but has grown into a Curse, a Thing. Every correction is a blood-bath which calls for new correction.

The truth stands ever beside God's throne
eternal: he who has wrought shall pay; that is law.
Then who shall tear the curse from their blood?
The seed is stiffened to ruin.

Clytaemestra answers, over the corpse of Agamemnon, that she has been bloody but the house is clean. No more evil need be done. Orestes is to make the same claim over the corpse of Clytaemestra herself. Both are mistaken.

The tragedy is no simple matter of right and wrong, of pride and fall, though these enter in. It is a matter of love and hate working simultaneously to force distorted action, and the situation is given depth by cross-characterization. Clytaemestra imagines before the chorus the scene in captured Troy, opening with savage satisfaction in the thought of what is going on and closing with a prayer for peace, that her husband and his men may use their victory temperately, so that no fresh wrong may follow. As she speaks these words, she is herself plotting the fresh wrong she deprecates. There is surface contradiction, but under it lies not only the fact that Clytaemestra is intensely proud of the husband she is about to murder but also the lyric imagination, akin to the diviner's gift, by which the character's mind can transcend time and distance and penetrate to a sphere of objective truth which is beyond the character's own desire and prejudice. When she tells Agamemnon and the public of the torments she went through in his absence at Troy, she is flattering him and misleading all, but by means of truth, not fiction. This is the past, and this is real.

It is evil and a thing of terror when a wife
sits in the house forlorn with no man by.

Flattery, confession, reproach combine (through how much longing for the memory-ghost, as with Menelaus for Helen, might Clytaemestra have gone before she took Aegisthus as a lover; or even after?). Agamemnon, on the point of being entangled by flattery and dragged to his death, soberly describes himself as proof against flatterers. In a sense this is irony; it corresponds to his entrance full of the pride of capture on the heels of a warning by the chorus against pride; to the gloomy speculations of the chorus on sackers of cities that presages the return of the herald to tell of Troy's obliteration. But that is mainly a matter of timing; here the point is that Agamemnon's intelligence is partly engaged with the course he does not mean to take. He is proof against illusions except at the one point where they will be fatal to him. When Aegisthus, in the height of his dispute with the challenging chorus (1668), says of Orestes,

> Exiles feed on empty dreams of hope. I know it. I
> was one,

the jibe turns into a flash of instantly forgotten sympathy. The actors, in particular Clytaemestra and the chorus, do not collide with purely external forces but act always against a part of their own will or sympathy which is committed to the other side, and what they kill is what they love.

The action of the play in itself, of the trilogy as a whole, is thus bound inward upon itself. Its course is not logical, not even strictly dramatic sequence. After the fashion of choral lyric, it is both united to itself and given inward dimension through persistent ideas and a complex of symbols.

Idea and Symbol

By "idea" I mean motive, theme of subject, or type of situation which is dominant in the dramatic action. By "symbol" I mean a particular thing, usually material, which may be taken to represent the idea. And by a "complex of symbols" I mean a group of such objects which are related to one another in their nature or use.

The exhaustive study of this technique and the detailing of its uses is a proper study for a monograph, not for a segment of the introduction to a translation.[10] I will content myself with illustrating the principle through the symbol-complex of the net.

A central motive in the *Oresteia* is the idea of entanglement: the taming of wild things, the subjugation of the powerful, the involvement of innocent creatures as well. It is expressed in the *curb* forged to subdue Troy (132) or Cassandra (1066); the *bit* that gags Iphigeneia (234); the *yoke* of circumstances that forces Agamemnon to his crime; the *yoke* of slavery forced on Troy (529), on Cassandra (953, 1071, 1226), on the defiant citizens (1635), even the yoke of teammates (842); the *snare* of the huntsman, in which Agamemnon captures Troy (358, 821) and Cassandra (1048) and in which he is presently captured (1115, 1375, 1611).[11] Curb, yoke, snare—different objects for related purposes—might have been no more than persistent and thematic metaphor, but they have one embodiment which is not metaphorical, and this is the robe or shawl in which Clytaemestra actually entangles Agamemnon in order to strike him down and which is to be displayed on stage as a murder exhibit by Orestes in *The Libation Bearers* (980–84, 997–1004). Clytaemestra anticipates herself when she tells of her dreams and imaginations of terror in Agamemnon's long absence (866–68):

> Had Agamemnon taken all
> the wounds the tale whereof was carried home to me,
> he had been cut full of gashes like a fishing net,

and returns to her imagery in her challenging confession of murder (1382–83):

---

[10] Miss Barbara Hughes is at present working on such a monograph as a doctoral dissertation.

[11] The idea of the manhunt appears in the retributive expedition against Troy (127, 695), and in *The Eumenides* it characterizes the Furies' pursuit of Orestes.

as fishermen cast their huge circling nets, I spread
deadly abundance of rich robes and caught him fast.

This is the idea seen in the thing and the thing embodying
the idea, both in metaphor and in action. There are numerous other symbols and other ideas. Symbols are the snake
(specially the viper) and the poison of the snake; the archer;
the house; the ship; gold. Ideas are (in addition to entanglement) persuasion (flattery); recurrent sickness; hate-in-love;
blood and sex; light in the dark; sound (of terror) in the
night; dream and memory. The bare lists are not complete,
and, in particular, neither symbols nor ideas are exclusive,
nor does a given symbol stand toward a given idea in a
one-to-one relation. The viper, who turns against his own
family, whose mating is murder, stands principally for the
idea of hate-in-love and, as such, might be called the prime
symbol of the *Oresteia*, but its poison is involved also in the
idea of recurrent sickness,[12] and its coils in the idea of
entanglement (elsewhere signified by yoke, net, etc., as we
have seen). So *The Libation Bearers*, 246–49:

> Behold
> the orphaned children of the eagle-father, now
> that he has died entangled in the binding coils
> of the deadly viper.

The spider web in which Agamemnon was trapped (1492) is
one more variation of entanglement, spun by another creature who murders in marriage. Entanglement may come by
outright force or by seduction and surprise. Clytaemestra
lures Agamemnon into it by flattery, persuasion, by her
sex (1116):

> Or is the trap the woman there, the murderess?

---

12 The word *palinkotos* might signify a sickness or poisoning which
lies hidden in the system, seemingly gone, then *re*curs; or the viper,
which *re*-coils upon itself, or those so close to it that they form a part
of itself.

Cross-binding and coherence of idea in symbol are seen where Agamemnon recoils (he is soon to surrender) from stepping on the gorgeous robe Clytaemestra has spread at his feet (922–27):

> Such state becomes the gods, and none beside.
> I am a mortal, a man; I cannot trample down
> these tinted splendors without fear thrown in my path.
> I tell you, as a man, not god, to reverence me.
> Discordant is the murmur at such treading down
> of lovely things.

On the level of discourse, the speech is moral. The male rationalism is fighting against the irrational persuasion of the woman, the Greek defends his code ("as if I were some Asiatic"), the king deprecates the subjects' disapproval; this is colored also by lyric memory. The "treading down of lovely things" recalls Paris, who "trampled down the delicacy of things inviolable" (371) and on whom Persuasion also worked (385). Agamemnon, who punished the barbarians, is being turned barbarian in order to be punished. He is a victim of his wife's flattery and the magnificence of his own possessions. Lastly, the robe itself on which he walks prefigures the robe in which he is to be entangled and killed.

Cut anywhere into the play, and you will find such a nexus of intercrossing motives and properties. The system gives the play its inner dimension and strength. An analogous but separable principle dominates the larger structure.

Dramatic Structure and Lyric Dimension

As theater, Agamemnon and its companion pieces are simple. The scene of Agamemnon is the familiar fixed position before the doors of a house, which is, as most often in subsequent drama and in the nature of things, a palace. The same setting serves for The Libation Bearers; The Eumenides has one of those shifts of scene which are relatively rare in

extant Greek tragedy, for we begin before the doors of
Phoebus at Delphi and end before the doors of Athene in
Athens, but this shift can easily be signified by addition or
subtraction of a very few properties.

Characters are used sparingly. Aeschylus has at his disposal the three actors who were by now allotted to each poet
or producer; but, far from reveling in this sober allowance,
he is most reluctant to use all three at once in speaking
action. Cassandra is on stage with Agamemnon and Clytaemestra, but does not speak until the other actors (not counting the chorus or chorus leader) have gone out.[13] Dialogue is,
for the most part, just that, a passage between two persons,
one of whom may be the chorus leader, at a time, not as in
modern drama a complex in which three, four, or a dozen

---

[13] Clytaemestra, apparently on stage at 83, does not respond to the
chorus at that point and remains silent through their stasimon (ode);
she speaks only when, 258–63, they address her again. In *The Libation
Bearers* Pylades, present almost through the entire play, speaks only
three lines (900–902); these have critical force in the action. In
Prometheus, the titan is silent all through the first scene, where he is
being fastened to the rock. We know also that Aeschylus exploited the
silent character in many of his lost plays. On the silent characters of
Aeschylus, see the scene in the *Frogs* of Aristophanes, where the ghost
of Euripides challenges that of Aeschylus in the presence of Dionysus
and Hades (911–22):

"*Eur.:* First of all he would cover a character's face and make him
      sit on the stage there,
      Achilles, maybe, or Niobe, but never show their features.
      They made his tragedy look fine, but didn't mutter a syllable.
"*Dion.:* By god, you know, they didn't at that.
"*Eur.:*   The chorus would pound out long chains
      of poetry, four one after another. The characters said nothing.
"*Dion.:* You know, I liked them quiet that way. They gave me as
      much pleasure
      as the ones that gabble at us now.
"*Eur.:*   Of course. You were a half-wit
      and that's a fact.
"*Dion.:*   I know, I know. Tell me then, why did he do it?
"*Eur.:* To lead you on, and keep the audience in suspense. They
      were waiting
      for Niobe to speak. Meanwhile his play was getting over.
"*Dion.:* The dirty rat! So all the time he was cheating us out of
      our drama.
      (*To Aesch.*) Why are you frowning and looking so cross?
"*Eur.:*   I'm exposing him. He doesn't like it."

speaking persons participate. There are supernumeraries to be sure, handmaidens attending Clytaemestra and soldiers returning with Agamemnon, the significant bodyguard of Aegisthus; and at the close of *The Eumenides* the stage is quite full of people, and the exodus takes on the dignity of a processional. Agamemnon clearly must enter with Cassandra beside him in a horse-drawn chariot. The unrolling of the robe for Agamemnon's feet is an effective use of showy gesture. Yet, on the whole, the trilogy is physically unpretentious, relying less on staging and properties than *Prometheus* appears to do. Also, it is physically static; not much physical activity or motion is called for. The use made of materials, of what might appeal to the eye, is measured and temperate.

There is a corresponding simplicity in plot. Considering the length of *Agamemnon*, there are few events that take place, nor are the major events displayed against any variety of subplot. It therefore takes dramatic time for these events to happen. The return of Agamemnon, assured from the watchman's opening speech (25), does not take place until line 782.[14] The only other *event* of the play is his

[14] Much unnecessary ingenuity has been wasted on the problem of "real" time in *Agamemnon*. By means of her beacons, Clytaemestra is understood to learn of Troy's capture just after the event, almost within the hour (320). The return voyage from Troy to Argos is a three or four days' sailing, hardly shortened by the hurricane that wrecked the fleet; and, further, Homer and the other sources on which tragedy drew make it plain that the Achaeans did not pick up and go home the moment Troy fell but understandably took some time getting off. Therefore, the arrival of the herald, followed by Agamemnon, comes days after the first scene of the play. This is true, but creates a problem only for those unduly preoccupied with the Aristotelian unities. "Tragedy tries as far as practicable to fall within the scope of a single day, or exceeds it by only a little" (*Poetics* v. 8). The statement of Aristotle is not made as if he meant to press it very hard. Also it should not be necessary, but apparently is, to point out that Aeschylus had never heard of Aristotle. To Aeschylus, the next thing that happened *in the plot*, after the arrival of the news, was the arrival of the Achaeans. It would have been, to him, as pointless as it would have been ugly to have the chorus solemnly quit the stage and return after the posting of a placard saying "six days later." What he does put in is a long choral lyric in which the choristers muse on the whole train of action (though not in chronological order) from the flight of Helen

22

murder, which does not take place until line 1344. Audience
and actors occupy the times preceding these events in a
growing strain of suspense, which gives the events redoubled
impact when at last they do take place. The means by which
the anomaly of many lines—little action is solved are the
same as the means by which action and motive are deep-
ened. The simplicity is on the surface. As, on its major
plane, the action of the tragedy moves deliberately forward,
in another dimension lyric memory and forecast take us, by
association of ideas rather than in obedience to order in
time, deep away into the past, the future, and the elsewhere.

Memory and forecast are a part of imagination, that
divining spirit which takes men beyond the limits of what
their senses can perceive. He who habitually, and under
patronage of a god, so divines is the *mantis* or prophet. The
prophet knew "all things that were, the things to come, and
the things past" (*Iliad* i. 70); that is, he knew not only past
and future, but *present*, what is occurring right now beyond
that fragmentary point of space where he stands. Calchas
the prophet of the Achaeans is remembered in the first ode,
Cassandra the prophetess of Troy appears in person. But,
apart from these formal prophets, the chorus assumes divining powers ("still by God's grace there surges within me
singing magic": "why this strain unwanted, unrepaid, thus
prophetic?"), and the imaginations of Clytaemestra, the
herald, Agamemnon, and Aegisthus range far away. Calchas,
in the memory of the chorus, goes deep into the past in order
to make predictions which will be fulfilled, years away, in
the subsequent action of the tragedy. Cassandra, who knows
of a past she never witnessed, sees in its light the invisible

to the fall of Troy; thus giving in lyric form the illusion that far
more time has passed than the real time it has actually taken them to
deliver their ode. At l. 475, after the lyric closes, they begin to speak
"in character." Their mood has changed; before the ode they were
utterly convinced by Clytaemestra's beacons; now they are unconvinced
and sarcastic. After the herald's speeches, they inform Clytaemestra
that she has been right all along, and she tells them she has done *her*
rejoicing *long ago*. By now, we are plainly meant to understand that a
lapse of time has occurred, but *not* encouraged to figure out just how
much, or how it could have happened.

network of treachery that waits for Agamemnon and her. The swan, who sings in the face of death and is helplessly dedicated to Apollo, is her symbol.

The choristers remember in their entrance chant the departure of the armament ten years ago (40–59), and it makes them see the struggle going on in Troy (60–68). They remember the portents that attended the gathering of the ships, the predictions of Calchas, and the sacrifice of Iphigeneia that was their sequel (104–257). Clytaemestra's living imagination follows the course of her beacon system, itself a device to defeat space and diminish time, as it breaks out from peak to peak on its way to her (281–316), and she sees the Achaeans in captured Troy, now, though far away (320–37). The chorus broods on the moral that Troy fallen conveys, but they think in pictures; of a man secure in wealth kicking over an altar (the audience will remember the golden Persians, their pride, sacrilege, and defeat); of Persuasion as a siren; of false fires and spurious metal gilded; of a greedy innocent child trying to catch a bird—the images, not the propositions, of delusion (367–95). This is Paris, and they fall at once to re-creating in imagination the flight of Helen (403–8). And there were *prophets* there, to be sure, who imagined the loneliness to follow for Menelaus with an empty bed and empty-eyed images of his wife, whose loveliness eluded him in dreams (408–26). But dream image is memory image, and there are others who remember too. The families of the common soldiers see brought back to them the ashes of their dead, transubstantiated by the money-changer, who is the god of war. They murmur against the king; their muttering is inarticulate and not clearly heard in high places but may be the symptom of a storm that waits for the returning king (427–74). *Te deum laudamus* has been transformed into foreboding, not through logical succession of ground and consequent but through a lyric succession of images whose forms melt into one another. Agamemnon's herald remembers the campaigning before Troy (551–81). At first, it is the dirty and brutal details of war-business that come out of the mist, but the sense of achievement infects him with Agamemnon's fatal pride, so that at the end the wings of his imagination take him out of the past across the present and far into the future and the days when the capture of Troy will be an antique glory of Argos. He is shaken out of this mood, however, by the questioning of the chorus leader, who wants to know what happened to the rest of the army and to Menelaus. He tells of the storm (650–70) in terms that make living things out of fire, wind, water, and rocks, and shows the wide seascape on which at dawn lay the wreckage of the Achaean fleet, torn flowers on the water.

The chorus, far now from the momentary exaltation they felt at news of the victory, now chant in terms of disaster: the sinister name of Helen, with the imagination once again of her flight to Troy (681–98); the lion's cub, the pet turned murderous (716–36), who is fatal Helen beguiling the Trojans (737–49). We remember Iphigeneia when Helen's eyes, like Iphigeneia's, sweep the beholder with soft arrows, and the victorious and guileful charmer recalls the innocent charmer who failed. The moralities which follow to prelude Agamemnon's entrance, the terms in which he is greeted, work again through images: houses gilded to hide dust, false coin, the smile of the charmer. Action follows in the public encounter of Clytaemestra and Agamemnon, but the wife's welcome brings back out of the past the fears that attended her during the years of separation (858–94). When he has gone into the house, the chorus turn uneasily from memory to forecast, and their gloom is abetted by Cassandra, who has vision on vision of the past, of the present (the intention behind Clytaemestra's face and words, the scene preparing behind closed doors), and the far future on the day when the avengers shall punish for the crime not yet committed (1069–1330). The death cry tells the chorus only what they already know. We do not see the murder take place, but we are told what happened (1381–92). In the scene that follows, where Clytaemestra faces the people, neither side can escape the memory of the hideous past which has forced these things to happen. Aegisthus' defense is a recounting of the crime of Atreus (1583–1611). At the end, Clytaemestra speaks as if all were over, but we know it is not, that the future holds more violence and it is the past which has made this so.

Lyric Tragedy

The brief dramatic time of the play is a point of convergence for actions that come from deep in the past and project far into the future. The limited stage is a pivotal point from which we can be transported far away. The tragedy of Agamemnon, Cassandra, and Clytaemestra is involved with and opens into the tragedy of the children of Thyestes, of Iphigeneia, of Troy and all the Achaean army; and its action, in return, is partly dictated by the figures never enacted, remote but always present in memory, of Atreus, Iphigeneia, Paris, and Helen.[15]

This is the form of lyric tragedy, perfected here and never since so completely realized. Its manner is due partly to the historical accident in which two forms of fiction were combined: drama, still relatively primitive and naïve, with choral lyric, now, after generations of mature practice, brought to its highest point of development by Simonides and Pindar. But the direction taken by this form is due also to deliberate choice. The desire is to transcend the limitations of dramatic presentation, even before these limitations have been firmly established. The spirit is that of Shakespeare's chorus in *Henry V*:

> But pardon, gentles all,
> The flat unraised spirits that have dared

---

[15] We may compare *The Persians*. The cast of actors consists only of Darius, his queen, Xerxes, messenger, and chorus. The visible scene in Persia is static. But the scene of the action which the play is *about* is Salamis, and then all the water and land between; the persons of this action are all the vast army of the Persians, and all the Greeks. *The Persians* is the great messenger-play.

> On this unworthy scaffold to bring forth
> So great an object: can this cockpit hold
> The vasty fields of France? Or may we cram
> Within this wooden O the very casques
> That did affright the air at Agincourt?

It is true that Shakespeare intends to take us to the actual
field of Agincourt, but principally he is aware of the impos-
sibility of *staging* expeditions and battles adequately, and
the appeal is to the imagination of the audience:

> For 'tis your thoughts that now must deck our kings,
> Carry them here and there; jumping o'er times,
> Turning the accomplishment of many years
> Into an hour-glass.

> Thus with imagined wing our swift scene flies
> In motion of no less celerity
> Than that of thought.

Shakespeare and Aeschylus alike forecast combinations
which only the motion picture can realize visually—flash-
back, imaginary scene, pictorial dramatization of history,
and messenger's account. Shakespeare's concern in this
particular play with the fragmentary nature of staged action
gives his chorus a brilliant part, but it is only a ghost of
Aeschylus, for in Aeschylus the past and the elsewhere
dominate present action.

But the direction in which he steered tragedy was not
generally followed. Sophoclean drama prevailed, since Euripides, under protest, framed tragedy in accordance with
Sophocles, not Aeschylus. Sophocles turned tragedy inward
upon the principal actors, and drama becomes drama of
character. His plays may open with public scenes, but, as
they progress, the interest focuses hard on the hero. *Oedipus
Tyrannus* begins with the plague in Thebes, but its ending is
all Oedipus, and Thebes is as good as forgotten. It is true

that the dead hand reaches out of the past to strike down Oedipus, Antigone, Aias, Heracles. But this is their tragedy, and theirs alone. *Agamemnon* is a play about the Trojan War, but *Antigone* is not a play about the Theban War, though that lies in the background. In Sophocles, the choruses are commentaries on the action, not part of the larger action, and their imagery is functional to the choruses themselves but not to the tragedy as a whole. Trilogy gives way to single drama. The enormous background becomes mainly irrelevant and is screened out. Lyric tragedy gives way to actor's tragedy.

Agamemnon is, in fact, the culmination of lyric tragedy, because the action narrows in *The Libation Bearers,* and when in *The Eumenides* it opens out again, it is with a new kind of meaning and composition.

"The Libation Bearers"

The second play of the trilogy takes place some years after the close of *Agamemnon.* The usurpers have grown secure in power. Orestes, sequestered in Phocis, is now a young man, and his sister Electra, resentful and bitter, awaits his return. The opening event is simple recognition, the identification of Orestes and the confirmation of the fact that, as Electra and the chorus hope, he means to avenge his father and regain his throne. Recognition is thus at once transformed into conspiracy. The children, with their faithful chorus, gather at Agamemnon's tomb, where Electra has gone on her mother's behalf, but without sympathy for her, to propitiate the dead king by reason of terrifying dreams which had shaken Clytaemestra in the night. The dead king is now a hero; his arrogance and his mistakes have been annulled by death, and his grave is a center of power. Therefore, the children with the chorus turn to him, invoke his ghost to anger against his murderers, with twofold driving intention: to enchant actual power out of the spirit and the grave and to incite themselves and arm themselves with the anger that will make them do what they must do. They then plot the means for assassination. Orestes poses as a traveling merchant who brings news of the death of Orestes; Clytaemestra, with archaic and stately courtesy, invites him in and sends for Aegisthus. As the messenger who is sent to summon him (she happens to be the slave who nursed Orestes when he was little) goes out on her errand, she encounters the chorus, who tell her not to suggest that Aegisthus should bring his bodyguard. Orestes and Pylades kill the king, and Clytaemestra stands at their mercy. She dares Orestes to kill her, and he stands irresolute until a word from Pylades solidifies his will. The bodies are brought out and displayed, with the robe in which Agamemnon had been entrapped, and Orestes declares publicly, as Clytaemestra had done, that this act is his own and that it is justice. But his wits are going, he sees the Furies, the avenging spirits of his mother (no one else can see them), and leaves in flight. This time, even before the play is over, the assassin knows that his act was not final but has created more suffering yet to come.

Once again the plot is simple, and the dramatic actions are few. Once again, despite these facts, the texture is saved from thinness, but the factors are different from those that give *Agamemnon* its coherence. First, this is a far shorter play. Second, the emphasis and direction have changed. We have, in a sense, more plot; there is intrigue, a practical problem. In *Agamemnon* the king's murder is felt by the witnessing chorus in their bones; it happens, is mourned, and defended. The problems of Clytaemestra, *whether* she can kill the husband she has loved and *how* she will do it, are implicit, but we are not present while she is solving them. But in *The Libation Bearers*, we are present at the deliberations of Orestes as he decides whether he can kill his mother, and how the assassination is to be effected. In recognition, decision, conspiracy, and climactic action we have, in fact, the mechanism, in naïve or even crude form, of that drama of revenge or play of successful action which we found in the Homeric story.

But *The Libation Bearers* is only superficially a drama of intrigue, and, in so far as it is one, it is hardly a significant specimen of its kind. The mechanism of the assassin's plot is simple, as the mechanism of recognition and identification is primitive. The emphasis lies on the mood in which the characters act.

For this is not a simple revenge play in which the young hero, long lost, returns to his sister and his kingdom to strike down the murderous and usurping villains. Orestes hardly gets a sight of his kingship before he must leave, haunted, driven, and alone. It is not until much later, near the close of *The Eumenides,* that he can speak as a king with subjects. Also, here the emotions of Orestes and Electra are, like those of Clytaemestra, half-committed to the side against which they act; and Clytaemestra, in turn, loves the son whom she fears, who kills her, and whom she would kill if she could. It is the *philos-aphilos* still, or love-in-hate, the murder committed not against an external enemy but against a part of the self.[16] The hate gains intensity from the strength of the original love when that love has been stopped or rejected. Electra ("the unmarried") has love to lavish, but her mother has turned it aside. The chorus, like the captive women they are, cling to the memory of Agamemnon, who enslaved them. Orestes, together with the sense of outrage over the loss of his rightful inheritance (the dynastic motive), nurses a deep sense of jealousy against his mother for having sacrificed not only Agamemnon but Orestes to her love for Aegisthus. The children were the price for which she bought herself this man (132–34). It is the venom of such jealousy that spills out in the bitterly salacious mockery of the dead lovers, and jealousy on his father's behalf and

---

[16] So *Hamlet* is transformed from the vigorous revenge-intrigue drama it might have been into the tragedy it is, because Hamlet is emotionally involved with the queen and Ophelia, who are on the side of the enemy. Even the arch-enemy is close in blood and perhaps once admired.

his own is the theme of his last sharp dispute with his mother. Clytaemestra, when she hears the false news of her son's death, is in a temper where relief and sorrow cross, though relief wins. Her very dream of bearing and nursing the snake (symbol of ingratitude), who fixes his poisonous fangs in her breast, enacts terror through a gesture of love. Aegisthus, at the word that Orestes is dead, goes soberly back to the image of the poison and the snake:

> For our house, already bitten
> and poisoned, to take this new load upon itself
> would be a thing of dripping fear and blood.

The chorus consider that both the tyrants are hypocrites, but even such hypocrites know what they are doing, and to whom.

This mood of tangled motivation means that the conspirators must work strongly upon themselves before they can act. Between the recognition and the resolve to act comes a scene of incantation. Sister, brother, and chorus turn to invoke dead Agamemnon. They implore his blessings and aid, they set forth their grievances and his, they challenge and taunt him to action:

Orestes
Think of that bath, father, where you were stripped of life.

Electra
Think of the casting-net that they contrived for you.

Orestes
They caught you like a beast in toils no bronzesmith made.

Electra
Rather, hid you in shrouds that were thought out in shame.

Orestes
Will you not waken, father to these challenges?

Electra
Will you not rear upright that best beloved head?

31

But, while they are invoking a power and a tradition whose force is felt but only dimly believed, they are also lashing themselves into the fury of self-pity that will make them do what they have to do. So the theme of lyric prophecy which was at work in *Agamemnon* is altered here. There is dealing in both cases with what lies beyond the powers of perception, but there it was lyric memory and vision on the part of those who were to witness, and so suffer from, the ugly act; here those who are themselves about to commit the ugly act manipulate the unseen, in a mood more of witchcraft than of prophecy.

For this reason and because the drama focuses on the will to act, *The Libation Bearers* ties back to *Agamemnon*, but *Agamemnon* ties back to the whole world of action latent behind the beginning of the tragedy. The symbols of the earlier play are caught up and intensified, particularly viper and net. But the emphasis is changed, because we see things from the point of view of the murderers. In *Agamemnon*, vice was alluring, wearing all the captivating graces of Helen and her attendant symbols; in *The Libation Bearers*, duty becomes repulsive. Both tragedies are carried on a strong underdrift of sex, but in the second play the sex impulse, though it works, has lost its charm. Orestes at the end has done a brutal, necessary job.

Like Clytaemestra at the close of *Agamemnon*, Orestes defends his position in terms of: "I have cleared my house. It was bloody, but necessary. Now we can have peace." As for Clytaemestra, his claim is no better than a desperate challenge flung at circumstances. The blood-bath was no cleaning-out, and it means more blood. Clytaemestra had to reckon with resentment in the state and the younger generation to come. The enlightenment of Orestes, the defeat of his hollow optimism, comes without delay. "The house has been rid of snakes": and at once, on the heads of his mother's Furies, more snakes appear.

"The Eumenides" (The Furies)

As we have seen (see above, p. 7), the last act of the trilogy finds Orestes cleared by Apollo but still pursued by the Furies. Is he clear, or not? Plainly, one divine decision has clashed with another decision which is also unquestionably divine. The fate of Orestes is referred to Athens and to a third divinity, Athene, who, reserving for herself the casting ballot, refers it to a jury of mortal men. When their vote is even and Athene has cast her deciding vote in his favor, the Furies must be propitiated by a new cult, as a new kind of goddess, in Athens. It is this episode that closes the play and the trilogy of the House of Atreus. The chorus has returned to its archaic part as chief character in the drama.

Who are the Furies, and what do they mean? And, since they stand up and identify themselves and protest their rights in the face of Apollo and Athene, we must also ask, What do these better-known Olympians represent for the purposes of Aeschylus?

As seen in the grand perspective, Agamemnon was only an unwilling agent in a chain of action far bigger than the fortunes of a single man. From the seduction of Atreus' wife, the murder of the children of Thyestes, the sacrifice of Iphigeneia and the youth of Hellas, claim and counterclaim have been fiercely sustained, each act of blood has been avenged in a new act of blood. The problems of public good have been solved through private murder, which is no solution, until the situation has become intolerable to the forces that rule the world, and these must intervene to see that the contestants and the impulses in nature which drive the contestants become reconciled and find their places in a scheme that will be harmonious and progressive, not purely destructive.

Behind the personal motivations in the two first dramas of the trilogy, we can, if we choose, discern a conflict of related forces: of the younger against the elder generation; of male against female; of Greek against barbarian. As the gods step out of the darkness, where, before, they could be reached only in fitful visions of the prophetic mind, and take their place on the stage, they personify these general forces, and, because they are divine and somewhat abstract, they can carry still further dimensions of meaning. The Furies are older than Apollo and Athene, and, being older, they are childish and barbarous; attached to Clytaemestra as mother, they are themselves female and represent the woman's claim to act which Clytaemestra has sustained from the beginning; in a Greek world they stand for the childhood of the race before it won Hellenic culture, the barbarian phase of pre-Hellenism, the dark of the race and of the world; they have archaic uprightness and strictness in action, with its attendant cruelty; they insist on the fact against the idea; they ignore the justifications of Orestes, for the blood on his hands means far more than the reasons why the blood is there. Apollo stands for everything which the Furies are not: Hellenism, civilization, intellect, and enlightenment. He is male and young. He despises cruelty for the fun of cruelty, and the thirst for blood, but he is as ruthless as the Furies. The commonwealth of the gods—therefore the universe—is in a convulsion of growth; the young Olympians are fighting down their own barbaric past.

But they must not fight it out of existence. In the impasse, Apollo uses every threat of arrogant force, but Athene, whose nature reconciles female with male, has a wisdom deeper than the intelligence of Apollo. She clears Orestes but concedes to the detested Furies what they had not known they wanted, a place in the affections of a civilized community of men, as well as in the divine hierarchy. There, gracious and transformed though they are, their place in the world is still made potent by the unchanged base of their character. The new city cannot progress by exterminating its old order of life; it must absorb and use it. Man cannot obliterate, and should not repress, the unintelligible emotions. Or again, in different terms, man's nature being what it is and Fury

34

being a part of it, Justice must go armed with Terror before it can work.

Thus, through the dilemma of Orestes and its solution, the drama of the House of Atreus has been transformed into a grand parable of progress. Persuasion (flattery), the deadly magic of the earlier plays, has been turned to good by Athene as she wins the Furies to accept of their own free will a new and better place in the world. By the time Orestes leaves the stage, he has become an issue, a Dred Scott or Dreyfus, more important for what he means than for what he is; and, when he goes, the last human personality is gone, and with it vanish the bloody entanglements of the House of Atreus, as the anonymous citizens of Athens escort their protecting divinities into the beginning of a new world.

It is appropriate, and characteristic of Aeschylus, that this final parable, with its tremendous burden of thought, should be enacted on the frame of a naïve dramatic structure, where the basis of decision on matricide is as crude as the base of Portia's decision against Shylock. The magnificence of *The Eumenides* is different from that of *Agamemnon*. The imagery—the lyric imagination in memory and magic—is gone, because we are not now merely to see but to understand. The final act comes down into the present day and seals within itself the wisdom, neither reactionary nor revolutionary, of a great man. But in its own terms *The Eumenides* is the necessary conclusion of a trilogy whose special greatness lies in the fact that it transcends the limitations of dramatic enactment on a scale never achieved before or since.

AGAMEMNON

CHARACTERS

Watchman

Clytaemestra

Herald

Agamemnon

Cassandra

Aegisthus

Chorus of Argive Elders

Attendants of Clytaemestra: of Agamemnon: bodyguard
of Aegisthus (all silent parts)

Time, directly after the fall of Troy.

AGAMEMNON

SCENE: *Argos, before the palace of King Agamemnon.*
The Watchman, who speaks the opening
lines, is posted on the roof of the palace.
Clytaemestra's entrances are made from a
door in the center of the stage; all others,
from the wings.

(*The Watchman, alone.*)

I ask the gods some respite from the weariness
of this watchtime measured by years I lie awake
elbowed upon the Atreidae's roof dogwise to mark
the grand processionals of all the stars of night
burdened with winter and again with heat for men,   5
dynasties in their shining blazoned on the air,
these stars, upon their wane and when the rest arise.

I wait; to read the meaning in that beacon light,
a blaze of fire to carry out of Troy the rumor
and outcry of its capture; to such end a lady's   10
male strength of heart in its high confidence ordains.
Now as this bed stricken with night and drenched
    with dew
I keep, nor ever with kind dreams for company:
since fear in sleep's place stands forever at my head
against strong closure of my eyes, or any rest: 15
I mince such medicine against sleep failed: I sing,
only to weep again the pity of this house
no longer, as once, administered in the grand way.
Now let there be again redemption from distress,
the flare burning from the blackness in good augury.   20

(A light shows in the distance.)

Oh hail, blaze of the darkness, harbinger of day's
shining, and of processionals and dance and choirs
of multitudes in Argos for this day of grace.
Ahoy!
I cry the news aloud to Agamemnon's queen,   25
that she may rise up from her bed of state with speed
to raise the rumor of gladness welcoming this beacon,
and singing rise, if truly the citadel of Ilium
has fallen, as the shining of this flare proclaims.
I also, I, will make my choral prelude, since   30
my lord's dice cast aright are counted as my own,
and mine the tripled sixes of this torchlit throw.

May it only happen. May my king come home, and I
take up within this hand the hand I love. The rest
I leave to silence; for an ox stands huge upon   35
my tongue. The house itself, could it take voice, might
    speak
aloud and plain. I speak to those who understand,
but if they fail, I have forgotten everything.

(Exit. The Chorus enters, speaking.)

Ten years since the great contestants   40
of Priam's right,
Menelaus and Agamemnon, my lord,
twin throned, twin sceptered, in twofold power
of kings from God, the Atreidae,
put forth from this shore   45
the thousand ships of the Argives,
the strength and the armies.
Their cry of war went shrill from the heart,
as eagles stricken in agony
for young perished, high from the nest   50
eddy and circle
to bend and sweep of the wings' stroke,
lost far below
the fledgelings, the nest, and the tendance.

Yet someone hears in the air, a god,   55
Apollo, Pan, or Zeus, the high
thin wail of these sky-guests, and drives
late to its mark
the Fury upon the transgressors.

So drives Zeus the great guest god
the Atreidae against Alexander:
for one woman's promiscuous sake
the struggling masses, legs tired,
knees grinding in dust,
spears broken in the onset.   65
Danaans and Trojans
they have it alike. It goes as it goes
now. The end will be destiny.
You cannot burn flesh or pour unguents,
not innocent cool tears,   70
that will soften the gods' stiff anger.

But we; dishonored, old in our bones,
cast off even then from the gathering horde,
stay here, to prop up
on staves the strength of a baby.   75
Since the young vigor that urges
inward to the heart
is frail as age, no warcraft yet perfect,
while beyond age, leaf
withered, man goes three footed   80
no stronger than a child is,
a dream that falters in daylight.

> (*Clytaemestra enters quietly. The Chorus*
> *continues to speak.*)

But you, lady,
daughter of Tyndareus, Clytaemestra, our queen:
What is there to be done? What new thing have you
    heard?
                                                        85
In persuasion of what

41

report do you order such sacrifice?
To all the gods of the city,
the high and the deep spirits,
to them of the sky and the market places,   90
the altars blaze with oblations.
The staggered flame goes sky high
one place, then another,
drugged by the simple soft
persuasion of sacred unguents,   95
the deep stored oil of the kings.
Of these things what can be told
openly, speak.
Be healer to this perplexity
that grows now into darkness of thought,   100
while again sweet hope shining from the flames
beats back the pitiless pondering
of sorrow that eats my heart.

I have mastery yet to chant the wonder at the
    wayside
given to kings. Still by God's grace there surges
    within me   105
singing magic
grown to my life and power,
how the wild bird portent
hurled forth the Achaeans'
twin-stemmed power single hearted,   110
lords of the youth of Hellas,
with spear and hand of strength
to the land of Teucrus.
Kings of birds to the kings of the ships,
one black, one blazed with silver,   115
clear seen by the royal house
on the right, the spear hand,
they lighted, watched by all
tore a hare, ripe, bursting with young unborn yet,
stayed from her last fleet running.   120
Sing sorrow, sorrow: but good win out in the end.

42

Then the grave seer of the host saw through to the
    hearts divided,
knew the fighting sons of Atreus feeding on the hare
with the host, their people.
Seeing beyond, he spoke: 125
"With time, this foray
shall stalk the castle of Priam.
Before then, under
the walls, Fate shall spoil
in violence the rich herds of the people.   130
Only let no doom of the gods darken
upon this huge iron forged to curb Troy—
from inward. Artemis the undefiled
is angered with pity
at the flying hounds of her father   135
eating the unborn young in the hare and the shivering
    mother.
She is sick at the eagles' feasting.
Sing sorrow, sorrow: but good win out in the end.

Lovely you are and kind   140
to the tender young of ravening lions.
For sucklings of all the savage
beasts that lurk in the lonely places you have
    sympathy.
Grant meaning to these appearances
good, yet not without evil.   145
Healer Apollo, I pray you
let her not with cross winds
bind the ships of the Danaans
to time-long anchorage   150
forcing a second sacrifice unholy, untasted,
working bitterness in the blood
and faith lost. For the terror returns like sickness to
    lurk in the house;
the secret anger remembers the child that shall be
    avenged."   155

43

Such, with great good things beside, rang out in the
  voice of Calchas,
these fatal signs from the birds by the way to the
  house of the princes,
wherewith in sympathy
sing sorrow, sorrow: but good win out in the end.

Zeus: whatever he may be, if this name   160
pleases him in invocation,
thus I call upon him.
I have pondered everything
yet I cannot find a way,
only Zeus, to cast this dead weight of ignorance   165
finally from out my brain.

He who in time long ago was great,
throbbing with gigantic strength,
shall be as if he never were, unspoken.   170
He who followed him has found
his master, and is gone.
Cry aloud without fear the victory of Zeus,
you will not have failed the truth: 175

Zeus, who guided men to think,
who has laid it down that wisdom
comes alone through suffering.
Still there drips in sleep against the heart
grief of memory; against   180
our pleasure we are temperate.
From the gods who sit in grandeur
grace comes somehow violent.

On that day the elder king
of the Achaean ships, no more
strict against the prophet's word,   185
turned with the crosswinds of fortune,
when no ship sailed, no pail was full,
and the Achaean people sulked
fast against the shore at Aulis
facing Chalcis, where the tides ebb and surge: 190

and winds blew from the Strymon, bearing
sick idleness, ships tied fast, and hunger,
distraction of the mind, carelessness
for hull and cable;   195
with time's length bent to double measure
by delay crumbled the flower and pride
of Argos. Then against the bitter wind
the seer's voice clashed out
another medicine   200
more hateful yet, and spoke of Artemis, so that the
    kings
dashed their staves to the ground and could not hold
    their tears.

The elder lord spoke aloud before them: 205
"My fate is angry if I disobey these,
but angry if I slaughter
this child, the beauty of my house,
with maiden blood shed staining
these father's hands beside the altar.   210
What of these things goes now without disaster?
How shall I fail my ships
and lose my faith of battle?
For them to urge such sacrifice of innocent blood   215
angrily, for their wrath is great—it is right. May all
    be well yet."

But when necessity's yoke was put upon him
he changed, and from the heart the breath came
    bitter
and sacrilegious, utterly infidel,   220
to warp a will now to be stopped at nothing.
The sickening in men's minds, tough,
reckless in fresh cruelty brings daring. He endured
    then
to sacrifice his daughter
to stay the strength of war waged for a woman,   225
first offering for the ships' sake.

45

Her supplications and her cries of father
were nothing, nor the child's lamentation
to kings passioned for battle.   230
The father prayed, called to his men to lift her
with strength of hand swept in her robes aloft
and prone above the altar, as you might lift
a goat for sacrifice, with guards
against the lips' sweet edge, to check   235
the curse cried on the house of Atreus
by force of bit and speech drowned in strength.

Pouring then to the ground her saffron mantle
she struck the sacrificers with   240
the eyes' arrows of pity,
lovely as in a painted scene, and striving
to speak—as many times
at the kind festive table of her father
she had sung, and in the clear voice of a stainless
    maiden   245
with love had graced the song
of worship when the third cup was poured.

What happened next I saw not, neither speak it.
The crafts of Calchas fail not of outcome.
Justice so moves that those only learn   250
who suffer; and the future
you shall know when it has come; before then, forget
    it.
It is grief too soon given.
All will come clear in the next dawn's sunlight.
Let good fortune follow these things as   255
she who is here desires,
our Apian land's singlehearted protectress.

(*The Chorus now turns toward Clytaemestra,
and the leader speaks to her.*)

I have come in reverence, Clytaemestra, of your
    power.

For when the man is gone and the throne void, his
  right
falls to the prince's lady, and honor must be given.   260
Is it some grace—or otherwise—that you have heard
to make you sacrifice at messages of good hope?
I should be glad to hear, but must not blame your
  silence.

Clytaemestra
As it was said of old, may the dawn child be born
to be an angel of blessing from the kindly night.   265
You shall know joy beyond all you ever hoped to
  hear.
The men of Argos have taken Priam's citadel.

Chorus
What have you said? Your words escaped my un-
  belief.

Clytaemestra
The Achaeans are in Troy. Is that not clear enough?

Chorus
This slow delight steals over me to bring forth tears,   270

Clytaemestra
Yes, for your eyes betray the loyal heart within.

Chorus
Yet how can I be certain? Is there some evidence?

Clytaemestra
There is, there must be; unless a god has lied to me.

Chorus
Is it dream visions, easy to believe, you credit?

Clytaemestra
I accept nothing from a brain that is dull with sleep.   275

Chorus
The charm, then, of some rumor, that made rich
  your hope?

Clytaemestra
Am I some young girl, that you find my thoughts so
silly?

Chorus
How long, then, is it since the citadel was stormed?

Clytaemestra
It is the night, the mother of this dawn I hailed.

Chorus
What kind of messenger could come in speed like
this?   280

Clytaemestra
Hephaestus, who cast forth the shining blaze from
Ida.
And beacon after beacon picking up the flare
carried it here; Ida to the Hermaean horn
of Lemnos, where it shone above the isle, and next
the sheer rock face of Zeus on Athos caught it up;   285
and plunging skyward to arch the shoulders of the
sea
the strength of the running flare in exultation,
pine timbers flaming into gold, like the sunrise,
brought the bright message to Macistus' sentinel
cliffs,
who, never slow nor in the carelessness of sleep   290
caught up, sent on his relay in the courier chain,
and far across Euripus' streams the beacon flare
carried to signal watchmen on Messapion.
These took it again in turn, and heaping high a pile
of silvery brush flamed it to throw the message on.   295
And the flare sickened never, but grown stronger yet
outleapt the river valley of Asopus like
the very moon for shining, to Cithaeron's scaur
to waken the next station of the flaming post.
These watchers, not contemptuous of the far-thrown
blaze,   300
kindled another beacon vaster than commanded.

48

The light leaned high above Gorgopis' staring marsh,
and striking Aegyplanctus' mountain top, drove on
yet one more relay, lest the flare die down in speed.
Kindled once more with stintless heaping force, they
send   305
the beard of flame to hugeness, passing far beyond
the promontory that gazes on the Saronic strait
and flaming far, until it plunged at last to strike
the steep rock of Arachnus near at hand, our watch-
    tower.
And thence there fell upon this house of Atreus' sons   310
the flare whose fathers mount to the Idaean beacon.
These are the changes on my torchlight messengers,
one from another running out the laps assigned.
The first and the last sprinters have the victory.
By such proof and such symbol I announce to you   315
my lord at Troy has sent his messengers to me.

Chorus
The gods, lady, shall have my prayers and thanks
    straightway.
And yet to hear your story till all wonder fades
would be my wish, could you but tell it once again.

Clytaemestra
The Achaeans have got Troy, upon this very day.   320
I think the city echoes with a clash of cries.
Pour vinegar and oil into the self-same bowl,
you could not say they mix in friendship, but fight
    on.
Thus variant sound the voices of the conquerors
and conquered, from the opposition of their fates.   325
Trojans are stooping now to gather in their arms
their dead, husbands and brothers; children lean to
    clasp
the aged who begot them, crying upon the death
of those most dear, from lips that never will be free.
The Achaeans have their midnight work after the
    fighting   330

that sets them down to feed on all the city has,
ravenous, headlong, by no rank and file assigned,
but as each man has drawn his shaken lot by chance.
And in the Trojan houses that their spears have
    taken
they settle now, free of the open sky, the frosts   335
and dampness of the evening; without sentinels set
they sleep the sleep of happiness the whole night
    through.
And if they reverence the gods who hold the city
and all the holy temples of the captured land,
they, the despoilers, might not be despoiled in turn.   340
Let not their passion overwhelm them; let no lust
seize on these men to violate what they must not.
The run to safety and home is yet to make; they
    must turn
the pole, and run the backstretch of the double
    course.
Yet, though the host come home without offence to
    high   345
gods, even so the anger of these slaughtered men
may never sleep. Oh, let there be no fresh wrong
    done!

Such are the thoughts you hear from me, a woman
    merely.
Yet may the best win through, that none may fail to
    see.
Of all good things to wish this is my dearest choice.   350

Chorus
My lady, no grave man could speak with better grace.
I have listened to the proofs of your tale, and I
    believe,
and go to make my glad thanksgivings to the gods.
This pleasure is not unworthy of the grief that gave
    it.
O Zeus our lord and Night beloved,   355
bestower of power and beauty,

you slung above the bastions of Troy
the binding net, that none, neither great
nor young, might outleap
the gigantic toils   360
of enslavement and final disaster.
I gaze in awe on Zeus of the guests
who wrung from Alexander such payment.
He bent the bow with slow care, that neither
the shaft might hurdle the stars, nor fall   365
spent to the earth, short driven.

They have the stroke of Zeus to tell of.
This thing is clear and you may trace it.
He acted as he had decreed. A man thought
the gods deigned not to punish mortals   370
who trampled down the delicacy of things
inviolable. That man was wicked.
The curse on great daring
shines clear; it wrings atonement   375
from those high hearts that drive to evil,
from houses blossoming to pride
and peril. Let there be
wealth without tears; enough for
the wise man who will ask no further.   380
There is not any armor
in gold against perdition
for him who spurns the high altar
of Justice down to the darkness.

Persuasion the persistent overwhelms him,   385
she, strong daughter of designing Ruin.
And every medicine is vain; the sin
smolders not, but burns to evil beauty.
As cheap bronze tortured   390
at the touchstone relapses
to blackness and grime, so this man
tested shows vain
as a child that strives to catch the bird flying
and wins shame that shall bring down his city.   395

51

No god will hear such a man's entreaty,
but whoso turns to these ways
they strike him down in his wickedness.
This was Paris: he came
to the house of the sons of Atreus,   400
stole the woman away, and shamed
the guest's right of the board shared.

She left among her people the stir and clamor
of shields and of spearheads,   405
the ships to sail and the armor.
She took to Ilium her dowry, death.
She stepped forth lightly between the gates
daring beyond all daring. And the prophets
about the great house wept aloud and spoke:
"Alas, alas for the house and for the champions,   410
alas for the bed signed with their love together.
Here now is silence, scorned, unreproachful.
The agony of his loss is clear before us.
Longing for her who lies beyond the sea
he shall see a phantom queen in his household.   415
Her images in their beauty
are bitterness to her lord now
where in the emptiness of eyes
all passion has faded."

Shining in dreams the sorrowful   420
memories pass; they bring him
vain delight only.
It is vain, to dream and to see splendors,
and the image slipping from the arms' embrace
escapes, not to return again,   425
on wings drifting down the ways of sleep.
Such have the sorrows been in the house by the
    hearthside;
such have there been, and yet there are worse than
    these.
In all Hellas, for those who swarmed to the host

the heartbreaking misery   430
shows in the house of each.
Many are they who are touched at the heart by these
    things.
Those they sent forth they knew;
now, in place of the young men
urns and ashes are carried home   435
to the house of the fighters.

The god of war, money changer of dead bodies,
held the balance of his spear in the fighting,
and from the corpse-fires at Ilium   440
sent to their dearest the dust
heavy and bitter with tears shed
packing smooth the urns with
ashes that once were men.
They praise them through their tears, how this man   445
knew well the craft of battle, how another
went down splendid in the slaughter:
and all for some strange woman.
Thus they mutter in secrecy,
and the slow anger creeps below their grief   450
at Atreus' sons and their quarrels.
There by the walls of Ilium
the young men in their beauty keep
graves deep in the alien soil
they hated and they conquered.   455

The citizens speak: their voice is dull with hatred.
The curse of the people must be paid for.
There lurks for me in the hooded night
terror of what may be told me.   460
The gods fail not to mark
those who have killed many.
The black Furies stalking the man
fortunate beyond all right
wrench back again the set of his life   465
and drop him to darkness. There among

53

the ciphers there is no more comfort
in power. And the vaunt of high glory
is bitterness; for God's thunderbolts
crash on the towering mountains.   470
Let me attain no envied wealth,
let me not plunder cities,
neither be taken in turn, and face
life in the power of another.

(*Various members of the Chorus, speaking severally.*)

From the beacon's bright message   475
the fleet rumor runs
through the city. If this be real
who knows? Perhaps the gods have sent some lie to
    us.

Who of us is so childish or so reft of wit
that by the beacon's messages   480
his heart flamed must despond again
when the tale changes in the end?

It is like a woman indeed
to take the rapture before the fact has shown for
    true.

They believe too easily, are too quick to shift   485
from ground to ground; and swift indeed
the rumor voiced by a woman dies again.

Now we shall understand these torches and their
    shining,
the beacons, and the interchange of flame and flame.   490
They may be real; yet bright and dreamwise ecstasy
in light's appearance might have charmed our hearts
    awry.
I see a herald coming from the beach, his brows
shaded with sprigs of olive; and upon his feet
the dust, dry sister of the mire, makes plain to me   495
that he will find a voice, not merely kindle flame

54

from mountain timber, and make signals from the
   smoke,
but tell us outright, whether to be happy, or—
but I shrink back from naming the alternative.
That which appeared was good; may yet more good
   be given.   500

And any man who prays that different things befall
the city, may he reap the crime of his own heart.

(*The Herald enters, and speaks.*)

Soil of my fathers, Argive earth I tread upon,
in daylight of the tenth year I have come back to
   you.
All my hopes broke but one, and this I have at last.   505
I never could have dared to dream that I might die
in Argos, and be buried in this beloved soil.
Hail to the Argive land and to its sunlight, hail
to its high sovereign, Zeus, and to the Pythian king.
May you no longer shower your arrows on our heads.   510
Beside Scamandrus you were grim; be satisfied
and turn to savior now and healer of our hurts,
my lord Apollo. Gods of the market place assembled,
I greet you all, and my own patron deity
Hermes, beloved herald, in whose right all heralds   515
are sacred; and you heroes that sent forth the host,
propitiously take back all that the spear has left.
O great hall of the kings and house beloved; seats
of sanctity; divinities that face the sun:
if ever before, look now with kind and glowing eyes   520
to greet our king in state after so long a time.
He comes, lord Agamemnon, bearing light in gloom
to you, and to all that are assembled here.
Salute him with good favor, as he well deserves,
the man who has wrecked Ilium with the spade of
   Zeus   525
vindictive, whereby all their plain has been laid
   waste.

Gone are their altars, the sacred places of the gods
are gone, and scattered all the seed within the
    ground.
With such a yoke as this gripped to the neck of Troy
he comes, the king, Atreus' elder son, a man   530
fortunate to be honored far above all men
alive; not Paris nor the city tied to him
can boast he did more than was done him in return.
Guilty of rape and theft, condemned, he lost the prize
captured, and broke to sheer destruction all the house 535
of his fathers, with the very ground whereon it stood.
Twice over the sons of Priam have atoned their sins.

Chorus
Hail and be glad, herald of the Achaean host.

Herald
I am happy; I no longer ask the gods for death.

Chorus
Did passion for your country so strip bare your
    heart?   540

Herald
So that the tears broke in my eyes, for happiness.

Chorus
You were taken with that sickness, then, that brings
    delight.

Herald
How? I cannot deal with such words until I under-
    stand.

Chorus
Struck with desire of those who loved as much again.

Herald
You mean our country longed for us, as we for
    home?   545

56

Chorus
So that I sighed, out of the darkness of my heart.

Herald
Whence came this black thought to afflict the mind
  with fear?

Chorus
Long since it was my silence kept disaster off.

Herald
But how? There were some you feared when the
  kings went away?

Chorus
So much that as you said now, even death were
  grace.   550

Herald
Well: the end has been good. And in the length of
  time
part of our fortune you could say held favorable,
but part we cursed again. And who, except the gods,
can live time through forever without any pain?
Were I to tell you of the hard work done, the nights   555
exposed, the cramped sea-quarters, the foul beds—
  what part
of day's disposal did we not cry out loud?
Ashore, the horror stayed with us and grew. We lay
against the ramparts of our enemies, and from
the sky, and from the ground, the meadow dews
  came out   560
to soak our clothes and fill our hair with lice. And if
I were to tell of winter time, when all birds died,
the snows of Ida past endurance she sent down,
or summer heat, when in the lazy noon the sea
fell level and asleep under a windless sky—   565
but why live such grief over again? That time is gone
for us, and gone for those who died. Never again
need they rise up, nor care again for anything.

Why must a live man count the numbers of the slain,
why grieve at fortune's wrath that fades to break
   once more?   570
I call a long farewell to all our unhappiness.
For us, survivors of the Argive armament,
the pleasure wins, pain casts no weight in the opposite scale.
And here, in this sun's shining, we can boast aloud,
whose fame has gone with wings across the land and
   sea: 575
"Upon a time the Argive host took Troy, and on
the houses of the gods who live in Hellas nailed
the spoils, to be the glory of days long ago."
And they who hear such things shall call this city
   blest
and the leaders of the host; and high the grace of
   God   580
shall be exalted, that did this. You have the story.

Chorus

I must give way; your story shows that I was wrong.
Old men are always young enough to learn, with
   profit.
But Clytaemestra and her house must hear, above
others, this news that makes luxurious my life.   585

(*Clytaemestra comes forward and speaks.*)

I raised my cry of joy, and it was long ago
when the first beacon flare of message came by night
to speak of capture and of Ilium's overthrow.
But there was one who laughed at me, who said:
   "You trust   590
in beacons so, and you believe that Troy has fallen?
How like a woman, for the heart to lift so light."
Men spoke like that; they thought I wandered in my
   wits;
yet I made sacrifice, and in the womanish strain
voice after voice caught up the cry along the city   595

to echo in the temples of the gods and bless
and still the fragrant flame that melts the sacrifice.

Why should you tell me then the whole long tale at
 large
when from my lord himself I shall hear all the story?
But now, how best to speed my preparation to   600
receive my honored lord come home again—what
 else
is light more sweet for woman to behold than this,
to spread the gates before her husband home from
 war
and saved by God's hand?—take this message to the
 king:
Come, and with speed, back to the city that longs
 for him,   605
and may he find a wife within his house as true
as on the day he left her, watchdog of the house
gentle to him alone, fierce to his enemies,
and such a woman in all her ways as this, who has
not broken the seal upon her in the length of days.   610
With no man else have I known delight, nor any
 shame
of evil speech, more than I know how to temper
 bronze.

(*Clytaemestra goes to the back of the stage.*)

Herald
A vaunt like this, so loaded as it is with truth,
it well becomes a highborn lady to proclaim.

Chorus
Thus has she spoken to you, and well you understand,   615
words that impress interpreters whose thought is
 clear.
But tell me, herald; I would learn of Menelaus,
that power beloved in this land. Has he survived
also, and come with you back to his home again?

59

Herald
I know no way to lie and make my tale so fair   620
that friends could reap joy of it for any length of
    time.

Chorus
Is there no means to speak us fair, and yet tell the
    truth?
It will not hide, when truth and good are torn
    asunder.

Herald
He is gone out of the sight of the Achaean host,
vessel and man alike. I speak no falsehood there.   625

Chorus
Was it when he had put out from Ilium in your sight,
or did a storm that struck you both whirl him away?

Herald
How like a master bowman you have hit the mark
and in your speech cut a long sorrow to brief stature.

Chorus
But then the rumor in the host that sailed beside,   630
was it that he had perished, or might yet be living?

Herald
No man knows. There is none could tell us that for
    sure
except the Sun, from whom this earth has life and
    increase.

Chorus
How did this storm, by wrath of the divinities,
strike on our multitude at sea? How did it end?   635

Herald
It is not well to stain the blessing of this day
with speech of evil weight. Such gods are honored
    apart.
And when the messenger of a shaken host, sad faced,

brings to his city news it prayed never to hear,
this scores one wound upon the body of the people;   640
and that from many houses many men are slain
by the two-lashed whip dear to the War God's hand,
   this turns
disaster double-bladed, bloodily made two.
The messenger so freighted with a charge of tears
should make his song of triumph at the Furies' door.   645
But, carrying the fair message of our hopes' salvation,
come home to a glad city's hospitality,
how shall I mix my gracious news with foul, and tell
of the storm on the Achaeans by God's anger sent?
For they, of old the deepest enemies, sea and fire,   650
made a conspiracy and gave the oath of hand
to blast in ruin our unhappy Argive army.
At night the sea began to rise in waves of death.
Ship against ship the Thracian stormwind shattered
   us,
and gored and split, our vessels, swept in violence   655
of storm and whirlwind, beaten by the breaking rain,
drove on in darkness, spun by the wicked shepherd's
   hand.
But when the sun came up again to light the dawn,
we saw the Aegaean Sea blossoming with dead men,
the men of Achaea, and the wreckage of their ships.   660
For us, and for our ship, some god, no man, by guile
or by entreaty's force prevailing, laid his hand
upon the helm and brought us through with hull
   unscarred.
Life-giving fortune deigned to take our ship in charge
that neither riding in deep water she took the surf   665
nor drove to shoal and break upon some rocky shore.
But then, delivered from death at sea, in the pale
   day,
incredulous of our own luck, we shepherded
in our sad thoughts the fresh disaster of the fleet
so pitifully torn and shaken by the storm.   670
Now of these others, if there are any left alive

they speak of us as men who perished, must they
   not?
Even as we, who fear that they are gone. But may
it all come well in the end. For Menelaus: be sure
if any of them come back that he will be the first.   675
If he is still where some sun's gleam can track him
   down,
alive and open-eyed, by blessed hand of God
who willed that not yet should his seed be utterly
   gone,
there is some hope that he will still come home
   again.
You have heard all; and be sure, you have heard the
   truth.   680

               (*The Herald goes out.*)

Chorus
Who is he that named you so
fatally in every way?
Could it be some mind unseen
in divination of your destiny
shaping to the lips that name   685
for the bride of spears and blood,
Helen, which is death? Appropriately
death of ships, death of men and cities
from the bower's soft curtained   690
and secluded luxury she sailed then,
driven on the giant west wind,
and armored men in their thousands came,
huntsmen down the oar blade's fading footprint   695
to struggle in blood with those
who by the banks of Simoeis
beached their hulls where the leaves break.

And on Ilium in truth
in the likeness of the name   700
the sure purpose of the Wrath drove
marriage with death: for the guest board

shamed, and Zeus kindly to strangers,
the vengeance wrought on those men
who graced in too loud voice the bride-song   705
fallen to their lot to sing,
the kinsmen and the brothers.
And changing its song's measure
the ancient city of Priam   710
chants in high strain of lamentation,
calling Paris him of the fatal marriage;
for it endured its life's end
in desolation and tears
and the piteous blood of its people.   715

Once a man fostered in his house
a lion cub, from the mother's milk
torn, craving the breast given.
In the first steps of its young life   720
mild, it played with children
and delighted the old.
Caught in the arm's cradle
they pampered it like a newborn child,
shining eyed and broken to the hand   725
to stay the stress of its hunger.

But it grew with time, and the lion
in the blood strain came out; it paid
grace to those who had fostered it
in blood and death for the sheep flocks,   730
a grim feast forbidden.
The house reeked with blood run
nor could its people beat down the bane,
the giant murderer's onslaught.
This thing they raised in their house was blessed   735
by God to be priest of destruction.

And that which first came to the city of Ilium,
call it a dream of calm
and the wind dying,
the loveliness and luxury of much gold,   740

the melting shafts of the eyes' glances,
the blossom that breaks the heart with longing.
But she turned in mid-step of her course to make
bitter the consummation,   745
whirling on Priam's people
to blight with her touch and nearness.
Zeus hospitable sent her,
a vengeance to make brides weep.

It has been made long since and grown old among
    men,   750
this saying: human wealth
grown to fulness of stature
breeds again nor dies without issue.
From high good fortune in the blood   755
blossoms the quenchless agony.
Far from others I hold my own
mind; only the act of evil
breeds others to follow,
young sins in its own likeness.   760
Houses clear in their right are given
children in all loveliness.

But Pride aging is made
in men's dark actions
ripe with the young pride   765
late or soon when the dawn of destiny
comes and birth is given
to the spirit none may fight nor beat down,
sinful Daring; and in those halls
the black visaged Disasters stamped   770
in the likeness of their fathers.

And Righteousness is a shining in
the smoke of mean houses.
Her blessing is on the just man.
From high halls starred with gold by reeking hands   775
she turns back
with eyes that glance away to the simple in heart,

64

ourning the strength of gold
amped false with flattery.   780
nd all things she steers to fulfilment.

(*Agamemnon enters in a chariot, with Cassandra
beside him. The Chorus speaks to him.*)

ehold, my king: sacker of Troy's citadel,
wn issue of Atreus.
Iow shall I hail you? How give honor   785
ot crossing too high nor yet bending short
f this time's graces?
'or many among men are they who set high
he show of honor, yet break justice.
f one be unhappy, all else are fain   790
o grieve with him: yet the teeth of sorrow
ome nowise near to the heart's edge.
ind in joy likewise they show joy's semblance,
nd torture the face to the false smile.
'et the good shepherd, who knows his flock,   795
he eyes of men cannot lie to him,
hat with water of feigned
ve seem to smile from the true heart.
ut I: when you marshalled this armament
or Helen's sake, I will not hide it,   800
1 ugly style you were written in my heart
or steering aslant the mind's course
o bring home by blood
acrifice and dead men that wild spirit.
ut now, in love drawn up from the deep heart,   805
ot skimmed at the edge, we hail you.
ou have won, your labor is made gladness.
sk all men: you will learn in time
rhich of your citizens have been just
a the city's sway, which were reckless.   810

gamemnon
o Argos first, and to the gods within the land,

65

I must give due greeting; they have worked with me
    to bring
me home; they helped me in the vengeance I have
    wrought
on Priam's city. Not from the lips of men the gods
heard justice, but in one firm cast they laid their
    votes   81
within the urn of blood that Ilium must die
and all her people; while above the opposite vase
the hand hovered and there was hope, but no vote
    fell.
The stormclouds of their ruin live; the ash that dies
upon them gushes still in smoke their pride of
    wealth.   82●
For all this we must thank the gods with grace of
    much
high praise and memory, we who fenced within our
    toils
of wrath the city; and, because one woman strayed,
the beast of Argos broke them, the fierce young
    within
the horse, the armored people who marked out their
    leap   82
against the setting of the Pleiades. A wild
and bloody lion swarmed above the towers of Troy
to glut its hunger lapping at the blood of kings.

This to the gods, a prelude strung to length of words.
But, for the thought you spoke, I heard and I re-
    member   83
and stand behind you. For I say that it is true.
In few men is it part of nature to respect
a friend's prosperity without begrudging him,
as envy's wicked poison settling to the heart
piles up the pain in one sick with unhappiness,   83
who, staggered under sufferings that are all his own,
winces again to the vision of a neighbor's bliss.
And I can speak, for I have seen, I know it well,

this mirror of companionship, this shadow's ghost,
these men who seemed my friends in all sincerity.   840
One man of them all, Odysseus, he who sailed un-
    willing,
once yoked to me carried his harness, nor went
    slack.
Dead though he be or living, I can say it still.

Now in the business of the city and the gods
we must ordain full conclave of all citizens   845
and take our counsel. We shall see what element
is strong, and plan that it shall keep its virtue still.
But that which must be healed—we must use medi-
    cine,
or burn, or amputate, with kind intention, take
all means at hand that might beat down corruption's
    pain.   850
So to the King's house and the home about the
    hearth
I take my way, with greeting to the gods within
who sent me forth, and who have brought me home
    once more.
My prize was conquest; may it never fail again.

    (Clytaemestra comes forward and speaks.)

Grave gentlemen of Argolis assembled here,   855
I take no shame to speak aloud before you all
the love I bear my husband. In the lapse of time
modesty fades; it is human.
                    What I tell you now
I learned not from another; this is my own sad life
all the long years this man was gone at Ilium.   860
It is evil and a thing of terror when a wife
sits in the house forlorn with no man by, and hears
rumors that like a fever die to break again,
and men come in with news of fear, and on their
    heels

another messenger, with worse news to cry aloud   865
here in this house. Had Agamemnon taken all
the wounds the tale whereof was carried home to me,
he had been cut full of gashes like a fishing net.
If he had died each time that rumor told his death,
he must have been some triple-bodied Geryon   870
back from the dead with threefold cloak of earth
    upon
his body, and killed once for every shape assumed.
Because such tales broke out forever on my rest,
many a time they cut me down and freed my throat   875
from the noose overslung where I had caught it fast.
And therefore is your son, in whom my love and
    yours
are sealed and pledged, not here to stand with us
    today,
Orestes. It were right; yet do not be amazed.
Strophius of Phocis, comrade in arms and faithful
    friend   880
to you, is keeping him. He spoke to me of peril
on two counts; of your danger under Ilium,
and here, of revolution and the clamorous people
who might cast down the council—since it lies in
    men's
nature to trample on the fighter already down.   885
Such my excuse to you, and without subterfuge.

For me: the rippling springs that were my tears have
    dried
utterly up, nor left one drop within. I keep
the pain upon my eyes where late at night I wept
over the beacons long ago set for your sake,   890
untended left forever. In the midst of dreams
the whisper that a gnat's thin wings could winnow
    broke
my sleep apart. I thought I saw you suffer wounds
more than the time that slept with me could ever
    hold.

68

Now all my suffering is past, with griefless heart   895
I hail this man, the watchdog of the fold and hall;
the stay that keeps the ship alive; the post to grip
groundward the towering roof; a father's single child;
land seen by sailors after all their hope was gone;
splendor of daybreak shining from the night of
     storm;   900
the running spring a parched wayfarer strays upon.
Oh, it is sweet to escape from all necessity!

Such is my greeting to him, that he well deserves.
Let none bear malice; for the harm that went before
I took, and it was great.
                         Now, my beloved one,   905
step from your chariot; yet let not your foot, my lord,
sacker of Ilium, touch the earth. My maidens there!
Why this delay? Your task has been appointed you,
to strew the ground before his feet with tapestries.
Let there spring up into the house he never hoped   910
to see, where Justice leads him in, a crimson path.

In all things else, my heart's unsleeping care shall
     act
with the gods' aid to set aright what fate ordained.

> (*Clytaemestra's handmaidens spread a bright
> carpet between the chariot and the door.*)

Agamemnon
Daughter of Leda, you who kept my house for me,
there is one way your welcome matched my absence
     well.   915
You strained it to great length. Yet properly to praise
me thus belongs by right to other lips, not yours.
And all this—do not try in woman's ways to make
me delicate, nor, as if I were some Asiatic
bow down to earth and with wide mouth cry out to
     me,   920
nor cross my path with jealousy by strewing the
     ground

69

with robes. Such state becomes the gods, and none
    beside.
I am a mortal, a man; I cannot trample upon
these tinted splendors without fear thrown in my
    path.
I tell you, as a man, not god, to reverence me.   925
Discordant is the murmur at such treading down
of lovely things; while God's most lordly gift to man
is decency of mind. Call that man only blest
who has in sweet tranquillity brought his life to
    close.
If I could only act as such, my hope is good.   930

Clytaemestra
Yet tell me this one thing, and do not cross my will.

Agamemnon
My will is mine. I shall not make it soft for you.

Clytaemestra
It was in fear surely that you vowed this course to
    God.

Agamemnon
No man has spoken knowing better what he said.

Clytaemestra
If Priam had won as you have, what would he have
    done?   935

Agamemnon
I well believe he might have walked on tapestries.

Clytaemestra
Be not ashamed before the bitterness of men.

Agamemnon
The people murmur, and their voice is great in
    strength.

Clytaemestra
Yet he who goes unenvied shall not be admired.

Agamemnon
Surely this lust for conflict is not womanlike?   940

Clytaemestra
Yet for the mighty even to give way is grace.

Agamemnon
Does such a victory as this mean so much to you?

Clytaemestra
Oh yield! The power is yours. Give way of your free
    will.

Agamemnon
Since you must have it—here, let someone with all
    speed
take off these sandals, slaves for my feet to tread
    upon.   945
And as I crush these garments stained from the rich
    sea
let no god's eyes of hatred strike me from afar.
Great the extravagance, and great the shame I feel
to spoil such treasure and such silver's worth of
    webs.

So much for all this. Take this stranger girl within   950
now, and be kind. The conqueror who uses softly
his power, is watched from far in the kind eyes of
    God,
and this slave's yoke is one no man will wear from
    choice.
Gift of the host to me, and flower exquisite
from all my many treasures, she attends me here.   955

Now since my will was bent to listen to you in this
my feet crush purple as I pass within the hall.

Clytaemestra
The sea is there, and who shall drain its yield? It
    breeds
precious as silver, ever of itself renewed,

the purple ooze wherein our garments shall be
dipped.   960
And by God's grace this house keeps full sufficiency
of all. Poverty is a thing beyond its thought.
I could have vowed to trample many splendors down
had such decree been ordained from the oracles
those days when all my study was to bring home
your life.   965
For when the root lives yet the leaves will come
again
to fence the house with shade against the Dog Star's
heat,
and now you have come home to keep your hearth
and house
you bring with you the symbol of our winter's
warmth;
but when Zeus ripens the green clusters into wine   970
there shall be coolness in the house upon those days
because the master ranges his own halls once more.

Zeus, Zeus accomplisher, accomplish these my
prayers.
Let your mind bring these things to pass. It is your
will.

> (*Agamemnon and Clytaemestra enter the
> house. Cassandra remains in the chariot.
> The Chorus speaks.*)

Why must this persistent fear   975
beat its wings so ceaselessly
and so close against my mantic heart?
Why this strain unwanted, unrepaid, thus prophetic?
Nor can valor of good hope   980
seated near the chambered depth
of the spirit cast it out
as dreams of dark fancy; and yet time
has buried in the mounding sand

the sea cables since that day   985
when against Ilium
the army and the ships put to sea.

Yet I have seen with these eyes
Agamemnon home again.
Still the spirit sings, drawing deep   990
from within this unlyric threnody of the Fury.
Hope is gone utterly,
the sweet strength is far away.
Surely this is not fantasy.   995
Surely it is real, this whirl of drifts
that spin the stricken heart.
Still I pray; may all this
expectation fade as vanity
into unfulfilment, and not be.   1000

Yet it is true: the high strength of men
knows no content with limitation. Sickness
chambered beside it beats at the wall between.
Man's fate that sets a true   1005
course yet may strike upon
the blind and sudden reefs of disaster.
But if before such time, fear
throw overboard some precious thing
of the cargo, with deliberate cast,   1010
not all the house, laboring
with weight of ruin, shall go down,
nor sink the hull deep within the sea.
And great and affluent the gift of Zeus
in yield of ploughed acres year on year   1015
makes void again sick starvation.

But when the black and mortal blood of man
has fallen to the ground before his feet, who then   1020
can sing spells to call it back again?
Did Zeus not warn us once
when he struck to impotence

that one who would in truth charm back the dead
    men?
Had the gods not so ordained   1025
that fate should stand against fate
to check any man's excess,
my heart now would have outrun speech
to break forth the water of its grief.
But this is so; I murmur deep in darkness   1030
sore at heart; my hope is gone now
ever again to unwind some crucial good
from the flames about my heart.

> (*Clytaemestra comes out from the house again
> and speaks to Cassandra.*)

Cassandra, you may go within the house as well,   1035
since Zeus in no unkindness has ordained that you
must share our lustral water, stand with the great
    throng
of slaves that flock to the altar of our household god.
Step from this chariot, then, and do not be so proud.
And think—they say that long ago Alcmena's son   1040
was sold in bondage and endured the bread of slaves.
But if constraint of fact forces you to such fate,
be glad indeed for masters ancient in their wealth.
They who have reaped success beyond their dreams
    of hope
are savage above need and standard toward their
    slaves.   1045
From us you shall have all you have the right to ask.

Chorus
What she has spoken is for you, and clear enough.
Fenced in these fatal nets wherein you find yourself
you should obey her if you can; perhaps you can not.

Clytaemestra
Unless she uses speech incomprehensible,   1050
barbarian, wild as the swallow's song, I speak
within her understanding, and she must obey.

74

Chorus

Go with her. What she bids is best in circumstance
that rings you now. Obey, and leave this carriage
    seat.

Clytaemestra

I have no leisure to stand outside the house and
    waste   1055
time on this woman. At the central altarstone
the flocks are standing, ready for the sacrifice
we make to this glad day we never hoped to see.
You: if you are obeying my commands at all, be
    quick.
But if in ignorance you fail to comprehend,   1060
speak not, but make with your barbarian hand some
    sign.

Chorus

I think this stranger girl needs some interpreter
who understands. She is like some captive animal.

Clytaemestra

No, she is in the passion of her own wild thoughts.
Leaving her captured city she has come to us   1065
untrained to take the curb, and will not understand
until her rage and strength have foamed away in
    blood.
I shall throw down no more commands for her con-
    tempt.

                    (*Clytaemestra goes back into the house.*)

Chorus

I, though, shall not be angry, for I pity her.
Come down, poor creature, leave the empty car. Give
    way   1070
to compulsion and take up the yoke that shall be
    yours.

                    (*Cassandra descends from the chariot
                        and cries out loud.*)

Oh shame upon the earth!
Apollo, Apollo!

Chorus
You cry on Loxias in agony? He is not
of those immortals the unhappy supplicate.   1075

Cassandra
Oh shame upon the earth!
Apollo, Apollo! ·

Chorus
Now once again in bitter voice she calls upon
this god, who has not part in any lamentation.

Cassandra
Apollo, Apollo!   1080
Lord of the ways, my ruin.
You have undone me once again, and utterly.

Chorus
I think she will be prophetic of her own disaster.
Even in the slave's heart the gift divine lives on.

Cassandra
Apollo, Apollo!   1085
Lord of the ways, my ruin.
Where have you led me now at last? What house
is this?

Chorus
The house of the Atreidae. If you understand
not that, I can tell you; and so much at least is true.

Cassandra
No, but a house that God hates, guilty within   1090
of kindred blood shed, torture of its own,
the shambles for men's butchery, the dripping floor.

Chorus
The stranger is keen scented like some hound upon
the trail of blood that leads her to discovered death.

Cassandra

Behold there the witnesses to my faith.   1095
The small children wail for their own death
and the flesh roasted that their father fed upon.

Chorus

We had been told before of this prophetic fame
of yours: we want no prophets in this place at all.

Cassandra

Ah, for shame, what can she purpose now?   1100
What is this new and huge
stroke of atrocity she plans within the house
to beat down the beloved beyond hope of healing?
Rescue is far away.

Chorus

I can make nothing of these prophecies. The rest   1105
I understood; the city is full of the sound of them.

Cassandra

So cruel then, that you can do this thing?
The husband of your own bed
to bathe bright with water—how shall I speak the
    end?
This thing shall be done with speed. The hand gropes
    now, and the other   1110
hand follows in turn.

Chorus

No, I am lost. After the darkness of her speech
I go bewildered in a mist of prophecies.

Cassandra

No, no, see there! What is that thing that shows?
Is it some net of death?   1115
Or is the trap the woman there, the murderess?
Let now the slakeless fury in the race
rear up to howl aloud over this monstrous death.

Chorus

Upon what demon in the house do you call, to raise
the cry of triumph? All your speech makes dark my
    hope.   1120
And to the heart below trickles the pale drop
as in the hour of death
timed to our sunset and the mortal radiance.
Ruin is near, and swift.

Cassandra

See there, see there! Keep from his mate the bull.   1125
Caught in the folded web's
entanglement she pinions him and with the black horn
strikes. And he crumples in the watered bath.
Guile, I tell you, and death there in the caldron
  wrought.

Chorus

I am not proud in skill to guess at prophecies,   1130
yet even I can see the evil in this thing.
From divination what good ever has come to men?
Art, and multiplication of words
drifting through tangled evil bring
terror to them that hear.   1135

Cassandra

Alas, alas for the wretchedness of my ill-starred life.
This pain flooding the song of sorrow is mine alone.
Why have you brought me here in all unhappiness?
Why, why? Except to die with him? What else could
  be?

Chorus

You are possessed of God, mazed at heart   1140
to sing your own death
song, the wild lyric as
in clamor for Itys, Itys over and over again
her long life of tears weeping forever grieves
the brown nightingale.   1145

78

Cassandra

Oh for the nightingale's pure song and a fate like
    hers.
With fashion of beating wings the gods clothed her
    about
and a sweet life gave her and without lamentation.
But mine is the sheer edge of the tearing iron.

Chorus

Whence come, beat upon beat, driven of God,   1150
vain passions of tears?
Whence your cries, terrified, clashing in horror,
in wrought melody and the singing speech?
Whence take you the marks to this path of prophecy
and speech of terror?   1155

Cassandra

Oh marriage of Paris, death to the men beloved!
Alas, Scamandrus, water my fathers drank.
There was a time I too at your springs
drank and grew strong. Ah me,
for now beside the deadly rivers, Cocytus   1160
and Acheron, I must cry out my prophecies.

Chorus

What is this word, too clear, you have uttered now?
A child could understand.
And deep within goes the stroke of the dripping fang
as mortal pain at the trebled song of your agony   1165
shivers the heart to hear.

Cassandra

O sorrow, sorrow of my city dragged to uttermost
    death.
O sacrifices my father made at the wall.
Flocks of the pastured sheep slaughtered there.
And no use at all   1170
to save our city from its pain inflicted now.
And I too, with brain ablaze in fever, shall go down.

Chorus
This follows the run of your song.
Is it, in cruel force of weight,
some divinity kneeling upon you brings   1175
the death song of your passionate suffering?
I can not see the end.

Cassandra
No longer shall my prophecies like some young girl
new-married glance from under veils, but bright and
    strong
as winds blow into morning and the sun's uprise   1180
shall wax along the swell like some great wave, to
    burst
at last upon the shining of this agony.
Now I will tell you plainly and from no cryptic
    speech;
bear me then witness, running at my heels upon
the scent of these old brutal things done long ago.   1185
There is a choir that sings as one, that shall not again
leave this house ever; the song thereof breaks harsh
    with menace.
And drugged to double fury on the wine of men's
blood shed, there lurks forever here a drunken rout
of ingrown vengeful spirits never to be cast forth.   1190
Hanging above the hall they chant their song of hate
and the old sin; and taking up the strain in turn
spit curses on that man who spoiled his brother's bed.
Did I go wide, or hit, like a real archer? Am I
some swindling seer who hawks his lies from door to
    door?   1195
Upon your oath, bear witness that I know by heart
the legend of ancient wickedness within this house.

Chorus
And how could an oath, though cast in rigid honesty,
do any good? And still we stand amazed at you,
reared in an alien city far beyond the sea,   1200

how can you strike, as if you had been there, the
  truth.

Cassandra
Apollo was the seer who set me to this work.

Chorus
Struck with some passion for you, and himself a god?

Cassandra
There was a time I blushed to speak about these
  things.

Chorus
True; they who prosper take on airs of vanity.　　　　1205

Cassandra
Yes, then; he wrestled with me, and he breathed
  delight.

Chorus
Did you come to the getting of children then, as
  people do?

Cassandra
I promised that to Loxias, but I broke my word.

Chorus
Were you already ecstatic in the skills of God?

Cassandra
Yes; even then I read my city's destinies.　　　　1210

Chorus
So Loxias' wrath did you no harm? How could that
  be?

Cassandra
For this my trespass, none believed me ever again.

Chorus
But we do; all that you foretell seems true to us.

Cassandra

But this is evil, see!

Now once again the pain of grim, true prophecy   1215
shivers my whirling brain in a storm of things
   foreseen.
Look there, see what is hovering above the house,
so small and young, imaged as in the shadow of
   dreams,
like children almost, killed by those most dear to
   them,
and their hands filled with their own flesh, as food
   to eat.   1220
I see them holding out the inward parts, the vitals,
oh pitiful, that meat their father tasted of. . . .
I tell you: There is one that plots vengeance for this,
the strengthless lion rolling in his master's bed,
who keeps, ah me, the house against his lord's return;   1225
my lord too, now that I wear the slave's yoke on my
   neck.
King of the ships, who tore up Ilium by the roots,
what does he know of this accursed bitch, who licks
his hand, who fawns on him with lifted ears, who like
a secret death shall strike the coward's stroke, nor
   fail?   1230
No, this is daring when the female shall strike down
the male. What can I call her and be right? What
   beast
of loathing? Viper double-fanged, or Scylla witch
holed in the rocks and bane of men that range the
   sea;
smoldering mother of death to smoke relentless hate   1235
on those most dear. How she stood up and howled
   aloud
and unashamed, as at the breaking point of battle,
in feigned gladness for his salvation from the sea!
What does it matter now if men believe or no?

What is to come will come. And soon you too will
    stand   1240
beside, to murmur in pity that my words were true.

Chorus
Thyestes' feast upon the flesh of his own children
I understand in terror at the thought, and fear
is on me hearing truth and no tale fabricated.
The rest: I heard it, but wander still far from the
    course.   1245

Cassandra
I tell you, you shall look on Agamemnon dead.

Chorus
Peace, peace, poor woman; put those bitter lips to
    sleep.

Cassandra
Useless; there is no god of healing in this story.

Chorus
Not if it must be; may it somehow fail to come.

Cassandra
Prayers, yes; they do not pray; they plan to strike,
    and kill.   1250

Chorus
What man is it who moves this beastly thing to be?

Cassandra
What man? You did mistake my divination then.

Chorus
It may be; I could not follow through the schemer's
    plan.

Cassandra
Yet I know Greek; I think I know it far too well.

Chorus
And Pythian oracles are Greek, yet hard to read.   1255

Cassandra

Oh, flame and pain that sweeps me once again! My
 lord,
Apollo, King of Light, the pain, aye me, the pain!
This is the woman-lioness, who goes to bed
with the wolf, when her proud lion ranges far away,
and she will cut me down; as a wife mixing drugs   1260
she wills to shred the virtue of my punishment
into her bowl of wrath as she makes sharp the blade
against her man, death that he brought a mistress
 home.
Why do I wear these mockeries upon my body,
this staff of prophecy, these flowers at my throat?   1265
At least I will spoil you before I die. Out, down,
break, damn you! This for all that you have done
 to me.
Make someone else, not me, luxurious in disaster. . . .
Lo now, this is Apollo who has stripped me here
of my prophetic robes. He watched me all the time   1270
wearing this glory, mocked of all, my dearest ones
who hated me with all their hearts, so vain, so wrong;
called like some gypsy wandering from door to door
beggar, corrupt, half-starved, and I endured it all.
And now the seer has done with me, his prophetess,   1275
and led me into such a place as this, to die.
Lost are my father's altars, but the block is there
to reek with sacrificial blood, my own. We two
must die, yet die not vengeless by the gods. For there
shall come one to avenge us also, born to slay   1280
his mother, and to wreak death for his father's blood.
Outlaw and wanderer, driven far from his own land,
he will come back to cope these stones of inward
 hate.
For this is a strong oath and sworn by the high gods,
that he shall cast men headlong for his father felled. 1285
Why am I then so pitiful? Why must I weep?
Since once I saw the citadel of Ilium
die as it died, and those who broke the city, doomed

by the gods, fare as they have fared accordingly,
I will go through with it. I too will take my fate.   1290
I call as on the gates of death upon these gates
to pray only for this thing, that the stroke be true,
and that with no convulsion, with a rush of blood
in painless death, I may close up these eyes, and rest.

Chorus
O woman much enduring and so greatly wise,   1295
you have said much. But if this thing you know be
    true,
this death that comes upon you, how can you, serene,
walk to the altar like a driven ox of God?

Cassandra
Friends, there is no escape for any longer time.

Chorus
Yet longest left in time is to be honored still.   1300

Cassandra
The day is here and now; I can not win by flight.

Chorus
Woman, be sure your heart is brave; you can take
    much.

Cassandra
None but the unhappy people ever hear such praise.

Chorus
Yet there is a grace on mortals who so nobly die.

Cassandra
Alas for you, father, and for your lordly sons.   1305
Ah!

Chorus
What now? What terror whirls you backward from
    the door?

Cassandra
Foul, foul!

Chorus
What foulness then, unless some horror in the mind?

Cassandra
That room within reeks with blood like a slaughter
  house.

Chorus
What then? Only these victims butchered at the
  hearth.   1310

Cassandra
There is a breath about it like an open grave.

Chorus
This is no Syrian pride of frankincense you mean.

Cassandra
So. I am going in, and mourning as I go
my death and Agamemnon's. Let my life be done.
Ah friends,   1315
truly this is no wild bird fluttering at a bush,
nor vain my speech. Bear witness to me when I die,
when falls for me, a woman slain, another woman,
and when a man dies for this wickedly mated man.
Here in my death I claim this stranger's grace of you.   1320

Chorus
Poor wretch, I pity you the fate you see so clear.

Cassandra
Yet once more will I speak, and not this time my own
death's threnody. I call upon the Sun in prayer
against that ultimate shining when the avengers strike
these monsters down in blood, that they avenge
  as well   1325
one simple slave who died, a small thing, lightly killed.

Alas, poor men, their destiny. When all goes well
a shadow will overthrow it. If it be unkind
one stroke of a wet sponge wipes all the picture out;
and that is far the most unhappy thing of all.   1330

(*Cassandra goes slowly into the house.*)

Chorus
High fortune is a thing slakeless
for mortals. There is no man who shall point
his finger to drive it back from the door
and speak the words: "Come no longer."
Now to this man the blessed ones have given   1335
Priam's city to be captured
and return in the gods' honor.
Must he give blood for generations gone,
die for those slain and in death pile up
more death to come for the blood shed,   1340
what mortal else who hears shall claim
he was born clear of the dark angel?

(*Agamemnon, inside the house.*)

Ah, I am struck a deadly blow and deep within!

Chorus
Silence: who cried out that he was stabbed to death
within the house?

Agamemnon
Ah me, again, they struck again. I am wounded twice.   1345

Chorus
How the king cried out aloud to us! I believe the
thing is done.
Come, let us put our heads together, try to find some
safe way out.

(*The members of the Chorus go about distractedly,
each one speaking in turn.*)

Listen, let me tell you what I think is best to do.
Let the herald call all citizens to rally here.

No, better to burst in upon them now, at once,   1350
and take them with the blood still running from their
blades.

I am with this man and I cast my vote to him.
Act now. This is the perilous and instant time.

Anyone can see it, by these first steps they have taken,
they purpose to be tyrants here upon our city.   1355

Yes, for we waste time, while they trample to the
    ground
deliberation's honor, and their hands sleep not.

I can not tell which counsel of yours to call my own.
It is the man of action who can plan as well.

I feel as he does, nor can I see how by words   1360
we shall set the dead man back upon his feet again.

Do you mean, to drag our lives out long, that we
    must yield
to the house shamed, and leadership of such as these?

No, we can never endure that; better to be killed.
Death is a softer thing by far than tyranny.   1365

Shall we, by no more proof than that he cried in pain,
be sure, as by divination, that our lord is dead?

Yes, we should know what is true before we break
    our rage.
Here is sheer guessing and far different from sure
    knowledge.

From all sides the voices multiply to make me choose   1370
this course; to learn first how it stands with Aga-
    memnon.

> (*The doors of the palace open, disclosing the
> bodies of Agamemnon and Cassandra,
> with Clytaemestra standing over them.*)

Clytaemestra
Much have I said before to serve necessity,
but I will take no shame now to unsay it all.
How else could I, arming hate against hateful men

disguised in seeming tenderness, fence high the nets 1375
of ruin beyond overleaping? Thus to me
the conflict born of ancient bitterness is not
a thing new thought upon, but pondered deep in time.
I stand now where I struck him down. The thing
    is done.
Thus have I wrought, and I will not deny it now. 1380
That he might not escape nor beat aside his death,
as fishermen cast their huge circling nets, I spread
deadly abundance of rich robes, and caught him fast.
I struck him twice. In two great cries of agony
he buckled at the knees and fell. When he was down 1385
I struck him the third blow, in thanks and reverence
to Zeus the lord of dead men underneath the ground.
Thus he went down, and the life struggled out of him;
and as he died he spattered me with the dark red
and violent driven rain of bitter savored blood 1390
to make me glad, as gardens stand among the showers
of God in glory at the birthtime of the buds.

These being the facts, elders of Argos assembled here,
be glad, if it be your pleasure; but for me, I glory.
Were it religion to pour wine above the slain, 1395
this man deserved, more than deserved, such sacra-
    ment.
He filled our cup with evil things unspeakable
and now himself come home has drunk it to the dregs.

Chorus
We stand here stunned. How can you speak this way,
    with mouth
so arrogant, to vaunt above your fallen lord? 1400

Clytaemestra
You try me out as if I were a woman and vain;
but my heart is not fluttered as I speak before you.
You know it. You can praise or blame me as you wish;
it is all one to me. That man is Agamemnon,
my husband; he is dead; the work of this right hand 1405

that struck in strength of righteousness. And that
is that.

Chorus
Woman, what evil thing planted upon the earth
or dragged from the running salt sea could you have
    tasted now
to wear such brutality and walk in the people's hate?
You have cast away, you have cut away. You shall go
    homeless now,   1410
crushed with men's bitterness.

Clytaemestra
Now it is I you doom to be cast out from my city
with men's hate heaped and curses roaring in my
    ears.
Yet look upon this dead man; you would not cross
    him once
when with no thought more than as if a beast had
    died,   1415
when his ranged pastures swarmed with the deep
    fleece of flocks,
he slaughtered like a victim his own child, my pain
grown into love, to charm away the winds of Thrace.
Were you not bound to hunt him then clear of
    this soil
for the guilt stained upon him? Yet you hear what I   1420
have done, and lo, you are a stern judge. But I say to
    you:
go on and threaten me, but know that I am ready,
if fairly you can beat me down beneath your hand,
for you to rule; but if the god grant otherwise,
you shall be taught—too late, for sure—to keep your
    place.   1425

Chorus
Great your design, your speech is a clamor of pride.
Swung to the red act drives the fury within your brain

signed clear in the splash of blood over your eyes.
Yet to come is stroke given for stroke
vengeless, forlorn of friends.   1430

Clytaemestra

Now hear you this, the right behind my sacrament:
By my child's Justice driven to fulfilment, by
her Wrath and Fury, to whom I sacrificed this man,
the hope that walks my chambers is not traced with
    fear
while yet Aegisthus makes the fire shine on my
    hearth,   1435
my good friend, now as always, who shall be for us
the shield of our defiance, no weak thing; while he,
this other, is fallen, stained with this woman you
    behold,
plaything of all the golden girls at Ilium;
and here lies she, the captive of his spear, who saw   1440
wonders, who shared his bed, the wise in revelations
and loving mistress, who yet knew the feel as well
of the men's rowing benches. Their reward is not
unworthy. He lies there; and she who swanlike cried
aloud her lyric mortal lamentation out   1445
is laid against his fond heart, and to me has given
a delicate excitement to my bed's delight.

Chorus

O that in speed, without pain
and the slow bed of sickness
death could come to us now, death that forever   1450
carries sleep without ending, now that our lord is
    down,
our shield, kindest of men,
who for a woman's grace suffered so much,
struck down at last by a woman.

Alas, Helen, wild heart   1455
for the multitudes, for the thousand lives
you killed under Troy's shadow,

you alone, to shine in man's memory
as blood flower never to be washed out. Surely a
   demon then   1460
of death walked in the house, men's agony.

Clytaemestra
No, be not so heavy, nor yet draw down
in prayer death's ending,
neither turn all wrath against Helen
for men dead, that she alone killed   1465
all those Danaan lives, to work
the grief that is past all healing.

Chorus
Divinity that kneel on this house and the two
strains of the blood of Tantalus,
in the hands and hearts of women you steer   1470
the strength tearing my heart.
Standing above the corpse, obscene
as some carrion crow she sings
the crippled song and is proud.

Clytaemestra
Thus have you set the speech of your lips   1475
straight, calling by name
the spirit thrice glutted that lives in this race.
From him deep in the nerve is given
the love and the blood drunk, that before
the old wound dries, it bleeds again.   1480

Chorus
Surely it is a huge
and heavy spirit bending the house you cry;
alas, the bitter glory
of a doom that shall never be done with;
and all through Zeus, Zeus,   1485
first cause, prime mover.
For what thing without Zeus is done among mortals?
What here is without God's blessing?

O king, my king
how shall I weep for you?   1490
What can I say out of my heart of pity?
Caught in this spider's web you lie,
Your life gasped out in indecent death,
struck prone to this shameful bed
by your lady's hand of treachery   1495
and the stroke twin edged of the iron.

Clytaemestra
Can you claim I have done this?
Speak of me never
more as the wife of Agamemnon.
In the shadow of this corpse's queen   1500
the old stark avenger
of Atreus for his revel of hate
struck down this man,
last blood for the slaughtered children.

Chorus
What man shall testify   1505
your hands are clean of this murder?
How? How? Yet from his father's blood
might swarm some fiend to guide you.
The black ruin that shoulders
through the streaming blood of brothers   1510
strides at last where he shall win requital
for the children who were eaten.

O king, my king
how shall I weep for you?
What can I say out of my heart of pity?   1515
Caught in this spider's web you lie,
your life gasped out in indecent death,
struck prone to this shameful bed
by your lady's hand of treachery
and the stroke twin edged of the iron.   1520

Clytaemestra
No shame, I think, in the death given

this man. And did he not
first of all in this house wreak death
by treachery?
The flower of this man's love and mine,   1525
Iphigeneia of the tears
he dealt with even as he has suffered.
Let his speech in death's house be not loud.
With the sword he struck,
with the sword he paid for his own act.

Chorus
My thoughts are swept away and I go bewildered.   1530
Where shall I turn the brain's
activity in speed when the house is falling?
There is fear in the beat of the blood rain breaking
wall and tower. The drops come thicker.
Still fate grinds on yet more stones the blade   1535
for more acts of terror.

Earth, my earth, why did you not fold me under
before ever I saw this man lie dead
fenced by the tub in silver?   1540
Who shall bury him? Who shall mourn him?
Shall you dare this who have killed
your lord? Make lamentation,
render the graceless grace to his soul   1545
for huge things done in wickedness?
Who over this great man's grave shall lay
the blessing of tears
worked soberly from a true heart?   1550

Clytaemestra
Not for you to speak of such tendance.
Through us he fell,
by us he died; we shall bury.
There will be no tears in this house for him.
It must be Iphigeneia   1555
his child, who else,
shall greet her father by the whirling stream

94

and the ferry of tears,
to close him in her arms and kiss him.

Chorus

Here is anger for anger. Between them   1560
who shall judge lightly?
The spoiler is robbed; he killed, he has paid.
The truth stands ever beside God's throne
eternal: he who has wrought shall pay; that is law.
Then who shall tear the curse from their blood?   1565
The seed is stiffened to ruin.

Clytaemestra

You see truth in the future
at last. Yet I wish
to seal my oath with the Spirit
in the house: I will endure all things as they stand   1570
now, hard though it be. Hereafter
let him go forth to make bleed with death
and guilt the houses of others.
I will take some small
measure of our riches, and be content
that I swept from these halls   1575
the murder, the sin, and the fury.

(*Aegisthus enters, followed at a little distance by his
                       armed bodyguard.*)

Aegisthus

O splendor and exaltation of this day of doom!
Now I can say once more that the high gods look
    down
on mortal crimes to vindicate the right at last,
now that I see this man—sweet sight—before me here   1580
sprawled in the tangling nets of fury, to atone
the calculated evil of his father's hand.
For Atreus, this man's father, King of Argolis—
I tell you the clear story—drove my father forth,
Thyestes, his own brother, who had challenged him   1585
in his king's right—forth from his city and his home.

Yet sad Thyestes came again to supplicate
the hearth, and win some grace, in that he was not
  slain
nor soiled the doorstone of his fathers with blood
  spilled.
Not his own blood. But Atreus, this man's godless sire,   1590
angrily hospitable set a feast for him,
in seeming a glad day of fresh meat slain and good
cheer; then served my father his own children's flesh
to feed on. For he carved away the extremities,
hands, feet, and cut the flesh apart, and covered them   1595
served in a dish to my father at his table apart,
who with no thought for the featureless meal before
  him ate
that ghastly food whose curse works now before
  your eyes.
But when he knew the terrible thing that he had done,
he spat the dead meat from him with a cry, and reeled   1600
spurning the table back to heel with strength the
  curse:
"Thus crash in ruin all the seed of Pleisthenes."
Out of such acts you see this dead man stricken here,
and it was I, in my right, who wrought th' murder, I
third born to my unhappy father, and w ch him   1605
driven, a helpless baby in arms, to banishment.
Yet I grew up, and justice brought me home again,
till from afar I laid my hands upon this man,
since it was I who pieced together the fell plot.
Now I can die in honor again, if die I must,   1610
having seen him caught in the cords of his just
  punishment.

Chorus

Aegisthus, this strong vaunting in distress is vile.
You claim that you deliberately killed the king,
you, and you only, wrought the pity of this death.
I tell you then: There shall be no escape, your head   1615
shall face the stones of anger from the people's hands.

Aegisthus

So loud from you, stooped to the meanest rowing
    bench
with the ship's masters lordly on the deck above?
You are old men; well, you shall learn how hard it is
at your age, to be taught how to behave yourselves.   1620
But there are chains, there is starvation with its pain,
excellent teachers of good manners to old men,
wise surgeons and exemplars. Look! Can you not
    see it?
Lash not at the goads for fear you hit them, and be
    hurt.

Chorus

So then you, like a woman, waited the war out   1625
here in the house, shaming the master's bed with lust,
and planned against the lord of war this treacherous
    death?

Aegisthus

It is just such words as these will make you cry in
    pain.
Not yours the lips of Orpheus, no, quite otherwise,
whose voice of rapture dragged all creatures in his
    train.   1630
You shall be dragged, for baby whimperings sobbed
    out
in rage. Once broken, you will be easier to deal with.

Chorus

How shall you be lord of the men of Argos, you
who planned the murder of this man, yet could not
    dare
to act it out, and cut him down with your own hand?   1635

Aegisthus

No, clearly the deception was the woman's part,
and I was suspect, that had hated him so long.
Still with his money I shall endeavor to control
the citizens. The mutinous man shall feel the yoke

drag at his neck, no cornfed racing colt that runs   1640
free traced; but hunger, grim companion of the dark
dungeon shall see him broken to the hand at last.

Chorus
But why, why then, you coward, could you not have
   slain
your man yourself? Why must it be his wife who
   killed,
to curse the country and the gods within the ground?   1645
Oh, can Orestes live, be somewhere in sunlight still?
Shall fate grown gracious ever bring him back again
in strength of hand to overwhelm these murderers?

Aegisthus
You shall learn then, since you stick to stubbornness
   of mouth and hand.
Up now from your cover, my henchman: here is work
   for you to do.   1650

Chorus
Look, they come! Let every man clap fist upon his
   hilted sword.

Aegisthus
I too am sword-handed against you; I am not afraid
   of death.

Chorus
Death you said and death it shall be; we take up the
   word of fate.

Clytaemestra
No, my dearest, dearest of all men, we have done
   enough. No more
violence. Here is a monstrous harvest and a bitter
   reaping time.   1655
There is pain enough already. Let us not be bloody
   now.
Honored gentlemen of Argos, go to your homes now
   and give way

to the stress of fate and season. We could not do
  otherwise
than we did. If this is the end of suffering, we can
  be content
broken as we are by the brute heel of angry destiny.   1660
Thus a woman speaks among you. Shall men deign
  to understand?

Aegisthus
Yes, but think of these foolish lips that blossom into
  leering gibes,
think of the taunts they spit against me daring
  destiny and power,
sober opinion lost in insults hurled against my
  majesty.

Chorus
It was never the Argive way to grovel at a vile man's
  feet.   1665

Aegisthus
I shall not forget this; in the days to come I shall be
  there.

Chorus
Nevermore, if God's hand guiding brings Orestes
  home again.

Aegisthus
Exiles feed on empty dreams of hope. I know it. I
  was one.

Chorus
Have your way, gorge and grow fat, soil justice, while
  the power is yours.

Aegisthus
You shall pay, make no mistake, for this misguided
  insolence.   1670

Chorus
Crow and strut, brave cockerel by your hen; you have
 no threats to fear.

Clytaemestra
These are howls of impotent rage; forget them, dearest; you and I
have the power; we two shall bring good order to our
 house at least.

(*They enter the house. The doors close. All persons
 leave the stage.*)

THE
LIBATION BEARERS

CHARACTERS

Orestes, son of Agamemnon and Clytaemestra

Pylades, his friend

Electra, his sister

Chorus, of foreign serving-women

A servant (doorkeeper)

Clytaemestra, now wife of Aegisthus, queen of Argos

Cilissa, the nurse

Aegisthus, now king of Argos

A follower of Aegisthus

*Various attendants of Orestes, Clytaemestra, Aegisthus
(silent parts)*

THE LIBATION BEARERS

SCENE: *Argos. The first part of the play (1–651) takes place at the tomb of Agamemnon: the last part (652 to the end) before the door of Clytaemestra's palace. No mechanical change of scene is necessary. The altar or tomb of Agamemnon should be well down stage. The door to the house should be in the center, back.*

(Enter, as travelers, Orestes and Pylades.)

Orestes

Hermes, lord of the dead, who watch over the powers
of my fathers, be my savior and stand by my claim.
Here is my own soil that I walk. I have come home;
and by this mounded gravebank I invoke my sire
to hear, to listen.   5
Here is a lock of hair for Inachus, who made
me grow to manhood. Here a strand to mark my grief.
I was not by, my father, to mourn for your death
nor stretched my hand out when they took your
    corpse away.

(The chorus, with Electra, enter from the side.)

But what can this mean that I see, this group that
    comes   10
of women veiled in dignities of black? At what
sudden occurrence can I guess? Is this some new
wound struck into our house? I think they bring
    these urns
to pour, in my father's honor, to appease the powers

below. Can I be right? Surely, I think I see   15
Electra, my own sister, walk in bitter show
of mourning. Zeus, Zeus, grant me vengeance for my
   father's
murder. Stand and fight beside me, of your grace.

Pylades, stand we out of their way. So may I learn
the meaning of these women; what their prayer
   would ask.   20

Chorus
I came in haste out of the house
to carry libations, hurt by the hard stroke of hands.
My cheek shows bright, ripped in the bloody furrows
of nails gashing the skin.   25
This is my life: to feed the heart on hard-drawn
   breath.
And in my grief, with splitting weft
of ragtorn linen across my heart's
brave show of robes
came sound of my hands' strokes   30
in sorrows whence smiles are fled.

Terror, the dream diviner of
this house, belled clear, shuddered the skin, blew
   wrath
from sleep, a cry in night's obscure watches,
a voice of fear deep in the house,   35
dropping deadweight in women's inner chambers.
And they who read the dream meanings
and spoke under guarantee of God
told how under earth
dead men held a grudge still   40
and smoldered at their murderers.

On such grace without grace, evil's turning aside
(Earth, Earth, kind mother!)
bent, the godless woman   45
sends me forth. But terror
is on me for this word let fall.

What can wash off the blood once spilled upon the
    ground?
O hearth soaked in sorrow,
o wreckage of a fallen house.   50
Sunless and where men fear to walk
the mists huddle upon this house
where the high lords have perished.

The pride not to be warred with, fought with, not to
    be beaten down   55
of old, sounded in all men's
ears, in all hearts sounded,
has shrunk away. A man
goes in fear. High fortune,
this in man's eyes is god and more than god is this.   60
But, as a beam balances, so
sudden disasters wait, to strike
some in the brightness, some in gloom
of half dark in their elder time.
Desperate night holds others.   65

Through too much glut of blood drunk by our foster-
    ing ground
the vengeful gore is caked and hard, will not drain
    through.
The deep-run ruin carries away
the man of guilt. Swarming infection boils within.   70

For one who handles the bridal close, there is no cure.
All the world's waters running in a single drift
may try to wash blood from the hand
of the stained man; they only bring new blood guilt on.   75

But as for me: gods have forced on my city
resisted fate. From our fathers' houses
they led us here, to take the lot of slaves.
And mine it is to wrench my will, and consent
to their commands, right or wrong,   80
to beat down my edged hate.
And yet under veils I weep

the vanities that have killed
my lord; and freeze with sorrow in the secret heart.

Electra
Attendant women, who order our house, since you
are with me in this supplication and escort   85
me here, be also my advisers in this rite.
What shall I say, as I pour out these outpourings
of sorrow? How say the good word, how make my
      prayer
to my father? Shall I say I bring it to the man
beloved, from a loving wife, and mean my mother? I   90
have not the daring to say this, nor know what else
to say, as I pour this liquid on my father's tomb.
Shall I say this sentence, regular in human use:
"Grant good return to those who send to you these
      flowers
of honor: gifts to match the . . . evil they have done."   95

Or, quiet and dishonored, as my father died
shall I pour out this offering for the ground to drink,
and go, like one who empties garbage out of doors,
and turn my eyes, and throw the vessel far away.

Dear friends, in this deliberation stay with me.   100
We hold a common hatred in this house. Do not
for fear of any, hide your thought inside your heart.
The day of destiny waits for the free man as well
as for the man enslaved beneath an alien hand.
If you know any better course than mine, tell me.   105

Chorus
In reverence for your father's tomb as if it were
an altar, I will speak my heart's thought, as you ask.

Electra
Tell me then, please, as you respect my father's grave.

Chorus
Say words of grace for those of good will, as you pour.

Electra
Whom of those closest to me can I call my friend?   110

Chorus
Yourself first; all who hate Aegisthus after that.

Electra
You mean these prayers shall be for you, and for myself?

Chorus
You see it now; but it is you whose thought this is.

Electra
Is there some other we should bring in on our side?

Chorus
Remember Orestes, though he wanders far away.   115

Electra
That was well spoken; you did well reminding me.

Chorus
Remember, too, the murderers, and against them . . .

Electra
What shall I say? Guide and instruct my ignorance.

Chorus
Invoke the coming of some man, or more than man.

Electra
To come to judge them, or to give them punishment?   120

Chorus
Say simply: "one to kill them, for the life they took."

Electra
I can ask this, and not be wrong in the gods' eyes?

Chorus
May you not hurt your enemy, when he struck first?

Electra
Almighty herald of the world above, the world

below: Hermes, lord of the dead, help me; announce
my prayers to the charmed spirits underground, who
    watch   125
over my father's house, that they may hear. Tell Earth
herself, who brings all things to birth, who gives
    them strength,
then gathers their big yield into herself at last.
I myself pour these lustral waters to the dead,
and speak, and call upon my father: Pity me;   130
pity your own Orestes. How shall we be lords
in our house? We have been sold, and go as wan-
    derers
because our mother bought herself, for us, a man,
Aegisthus, he who helped her hand to cut you down.
Now I am what a slave is, and Orestes lives   135
outcast from his great properties, while they go proud
in the high style and luxury of what you worked
to win. By some good fortune let Orestes come
back home. Such is my prayer, my father. Hear me;
    hear.

And for myself, grant that I be more temperate   140
of heart than my mother; that I act with purer hand.

Such are my prayers for us; but for our enemies,
father, I pray that your avenger come, that they
who killed you shall be killed in turn, as they deserve.
Between my prayer for good and prayer for good I set   145
this prayer for evil; and I speak it against Them.
For us, bring blessings up into the world. Let Earth
and conquering Justice, and all gods beside, give aid.

Such are my prayers; and over them I pour these drink
offerings. Yours the strain now, yours to make them
    flower   150
with mourning song, and incantation for the dead.

Chorus
Let the tear fall, that clashes as it dies
as died our fallen lord;
die on this mound that fences good from evil,

washing away the death stain accursed   155
of drink offerings shed. Hear me, oh hear, my lord,
majesty hear me from your dark heart; oh hear.
Let one come, in strength
of spear, some man at arms who will set free the
     house   160
holding the Scythian bow backbent in his hands,
a barbarous god of war spattering arrows
or closing to slash, with sword hilted fast to his hand.

Electra
Father, the earth has drunk my offerings poured
     to you.
Something has happened here, my women. Help me   165

Chorus
Speak, if you will. My heart is in a dance of fear.

Electra
Someone has cut a strand of hair and laid it on
the tomb.

Chorus
          What man? Or was it some deep-waisted girl?

Electra
There is a mark, which makes it plain for any
     to guess.   170

Chorus
Explain, and let your youth instruct my elder age.

Electra
No one could have cut off this strand, except myself.

Chorus
Those others, whom it would have become, are full of
     hate.

Electra
Yet here it is, and for appearance matches well . . .

Chorus
With whose hair? Tell me. This is what I long to
know. . . .   175

Electra
With my own hair. It is almost exactly like.

Chorus
Can it then be a secret gift from Orestes?

Electra
It seems that it must be nobody's hair but his.

Chorus
Did Orestes dare to come back here? How could this
be?

Electra
He sent this severed strand, to do my father grace.   180

Chorus
It will not stop my tears if you are right. You mean
that he can never again set foot upon this land.

Electra
The bitter wash has surged upon my heart as well.
I am struck through, as by the cross-stab of a sword,
and from my eyes the thirsty and unguarded drops   185
burst in a storm of tears like winter rain, as I
look on this strand of hair. How could I think some
other
man, some burgess, could ever go grand in hair like
this?
She never could have cut it, she who murdered him
and is my mother, but no mother in her heart   190
which has assumed God's hate and hates her children. No.
And yet, how can I say in open outright confidence
this is a treasured token from the best beloved
of men to me, Orestes? Does hope fawn on me?
Ah

I wish it had the kind voice of a messenger   195
so that my mind would not be torn in two, I not
shaken, but it could tell me plain to throw this strand
away as vile, if it was cut from a hated head,
or like a brother could have mourned with me,
   and been
a treasured splendor for my father, and his grave.   200

The gods know, and we call upon the gods; they know
how we are spun in circles like seafarers, in
what storms. But if we are to win, and our ship live,
from one small seed could burgeon an enormous tree.

But see, here is another sign. Footprints are here.   205
The feet that made them are alike, and look like
   mine.
There are two sets of footprints: of the man who gave
his hair, and one who shared the road with him. I step
where he has stepped, and heelmarks, and the space
   between
his heel and toe are like the prints I make. Oh, this   210
is torment, and my wits are going.

    (*Orestes comes from his place of concealment.*)

Orestes
Pray for what is to come, and tell the gods that they
have brought your former prayers to pass. Pray for
   success.

Electra
Upon what ground? What have I won yet from
   the gods?

Orestes
You have come in sight of all you long since prayed
   to see.   215

Electra
How did you know what man was subject of my
   prayer?

Orestes
I know about Orestes, how he stirred your heart.

Electra
Yes; but how am I given an answer to my prayers?

Orestes
Look at me. Look for no one closer to you than I.

Electra
Is this some net of treachery, friend, you catch me in?   220

Orestes
Then I must be contriving plots against myself.

Electra
It is your pleasure to laugh at my unhappiness.

Orestes
I only mock my own then, if I laugh at you.

Electra
Are you really Orestes? Can I call you by that name?

Orestes
You see my actual self and are slow to learn. And yet   225
you saw this strand of hair I cut in sign of grief
and shuddered with excitement, for you thought you
    saw
me, and again when you were measuring my tracks.
Now lay the severed strand against where it was cut
and see how well your brother's hair matches my head.   230
Look at this piece of weaving, the work of your hand
with its blade strokes and figured design of beasts.
    No, no,
control yourself, and do not lose your head for joy.
I know those nearest to us hate us bitterly.

Electra
O dearest, treasured darling of my father's house,   235
hope of the seed of our salvation, wept for, trust
your strength of hand, and win your father's house
    again.

O bright beloved presence, you bring back four lives
to me. To call you father is constraint of fact,
and all the love I could have borne my mother turns   240
your way, while she is loathed as she deserves; my love
for a pitilessly slaughtered sister turns to you.
And now you were my steadfast brother after all.
You alone bring me honor; but let Force, and Right,
and Zeus almighty, third with them, be on your side.   245

Orestes
Zeus, Zeus, direct all that we try to do. Behold
the orphaned children of the eagle-father, now
that he has died entangled in the binding coils
of the deadly viper, and the young he left behind
are worn with hunger of starvation, not full grown   250
to bring their shelter slain food, as their father did.
I, with my sister, whom I name, Electra here,
stand in your sight, children whose father is lost.
  We both
are driven from the house that should be ours. If you
destroy these fledgelings of a father who gave you   255
sacrifice and high honor, from what hand like his
shall you be given the sacred feast which is your
  right?
Destroy the eagle's brood, and you have no more
  means
to send your signs to mortals for their strong belief;
nor, if the stump rot through on this baronial tree,   260
shall it sustain your altars on sacrificial days.
Safe keep it: from a little thing you can raise up
a house to grandeur, though it now seem overthrown.

Chorus
O children, silence! Saviors of your father's house,
be silent, children. Otherwise someone may hear   265
and for mere love of gossip carry news of all
you do, to those in power, to those I long to see
some day as corpses in the leaking pitch and flame.

Orestes
The big strength of Apollo's oracle will not
forsake me. For he charged me to win through this
    hazard,   270
with divination of much, and speech articulate,
the winters of disaster under the warm heart
were I to fail against my father's murderers;
told me to cut them down in their own fashion, turn
to the bull's fury in the loss of my estates.   275
He said that else I must myself pay penalty
with my own life, and suffer much sad punishment;
spoke of the angers that come out of the ground from
    those
beneath who turn against men; spoke of sicknesses,
ulcers that ride upon the flesh, and cling, and with   280
wild teeth eat away the natural tissue, how on this
disease shall grow in turn a leprous fur. He spoke
of other ways again by which the avengers might
attack, brought to fulfilment from my father's blood.
For the dark arrow of the dead men underground   285
from those within my blood who fell and turn to call
upon me; madness and empty terror in the night
on one who sees clear and whose eyes move in the
    dark,
must tear him loose and shake him until, with all
    his bulk
degraded by the bronze-loaded lash, he lose his city.   290
And such as he can have no share in the communal
    bowl
allowed them, no cup filled for friends to drink. The
    wrath
of the father comes unseen on them to drive them back
from altars. None can take them in nor shelter them.
Dishonored and unloved by all the man must die   295
at last, shrunken and wasted away in painful death.

Shall I not trust such oracles as this? Or if
I do not trust them, here is work that must be done.

Here numerous desires converge to drive me on:
the god's urgency and my father's passion, and   300
with these the loss of my estates wears hard on me;
the thought that these my citizens, most high re-
    nowned
of men, who toppled Troy in show of courage, must
go subject to this brace of women; since his heart
is female; or, if it be not, that soon will show.   305

Chorus

Almighty Destinies, by the will
    Zeus let these things
be done, in the turning of Justice.
For the word of hatred spoken, let hate
be a word fulfilled. The spirit of Right   310
cries out aloud and extracts atonement
due: blood stroke for the stroke of blood
shall be paid. Who acts, shall endure. So speaks
the voice of the age-old wisdom.

Orestes

Father, o my dread father, what thing   315
can I say, can I accomplish
from this far place where I stand, to mark
and reach you there in your chamber
with light that will match your dark?
Yet it is called an action   320
of grace to mourn in style for the house,
once great, of the sons of Atreus.

Chorus

Child, when the fire burns
and tears with teeth at the dead man
it can not wear out the heart of will.   325
He shows his wrath in the after-
days. One dies, and is dirged.
Light falls on the man who killed him.
He is hunted down by the deathsong
for sires slain and for fathers,   330
disturbed, and stern, and enormous.

Electra
Hear me, my father; hear in turn
all the tears of my sorrows.
Two children stand at your tomb to sing
the burden of your death chant.   335
Your grave is shelter to suppliants,
shelter to the outdriven.
What here is good; what escape from grief?
Can we outwrestle disaster?

Chorus
Yet from such as this the god, if he will,   34
can work out strains that are fairer.
For dirges chanted over the grave
the winner's song in the lordly house;
bring home to new arms the beloved.

Orestes
If only at Ilium,   345
father, and by some Lycian's hands
you had gone down at the spear's stroke,
you would have left high fame in your house,
in the going forth of your children
eyes' admiration;   350
founded the deep piled bank of earth
for grave by the doubled water
with light lift for your household;

Chorus
loved then by those he loved
down there beneath the ground   355
who died as heroes, he would have held
state, and a lord's majesty,
vassal only to those most great,
the Kings of the under darkness.
For he was King on earth when he lived   360
over those whose hands held power of life
and death, and the staff of authority.

Electra

No, but not under Troy's
ramparts, father, should you have died,
nor, with the rest of the spearstruck hordes   365
have found your grave by Scamandrus' crossing.
Sooner, his murderers
should have been killed, as he was,
by those they loved, and have found their death,
and men remote from this outrage   370
had heard the distant story.

Chorus

Child, child, you are dreaming, since dreaming is a
    light
pastime, of fortune more golden than gold
or the Blessed Ones north of the North Wind.
But the stroke of the twofold lash is pounding   375
close, and powers gather under ground
to give aid. The hands of those who are lords
are unclean, and these are accursed.
Power grows on the side of the children.

Orestes

This cry has come to your ear   380
like a deep driven arrow.
Zeus, Zeus, force up from below
ground the delayed destruction
on the hard heart and the daring
hand, for the right of our fathers.   385

Chorus

May I claim right to close the deathsong
chanted in glory across
the man speared and the woman
dying. Why darken what deep within me forever
flitters? Long since against the heart's   390
stem a bitter wind has blown
thin anger and burdened hatred.

Electra

May Zeus, from all shoulder's strength,

pound down his fist upon them,   395
ohay, smash their heads.
Let the land once more believe.
There has been wrong done. I ask for right.
Hear me, Earth. Hear me, grandeurs of Darkness.

Chorus
It is but law that when the red drops have been spilled   400
upon the ground they cry aloud for fresh
blood. For the death act calls out on Fury
to bring out of those who were slain before
new ruin on ruin accomplished.

Orestes
Hear me, you lordships of the world below.   405
Behold in assembled power, curses come from the
    dead,
behold the last of the sons of Atreus, foundering
lost, without future, cast
from house and right. O god, where shall we turn?

Chorus
The heart jumped in me once again   410
to hear this unhappy prayer.
I was disconsolate then
and the deep heart within
darkened to hear you speak it.
But when strength came back hope lifted   415
me again, and the sorrow
was gone and the light was on me.

Electra
Of what thing can we speak, and strike more close,
than of the sorrows they who bore us have given?
So let her fawn if she likes. It softens not.   420
For we are bloody like the wolf
and savage born from the savage mother.

Chorus
I struck my breast in the stroke-style of the Arian,

the Cissian mourning woman,
and the hail-beat of the drifting fists was there to see   425
as the rising pace went in a pattern of blows
downward and upward until the crashing strokes
played on my hammered, my all-stricken head.

Electra
O cruel, cruel
all daring mother, in cruel processional   430
with all his citizens gone,
with all sorrow for him forgotten
you dared bury your unbewept lord.

Orestes
O all unworthy of him, that you tell me.
Shall she not pay for this dishonor   435
for all the immortals,
for all my own hands can do?
Let me but take her life and die for it.

Chorus
Know then, they hobbled him beneath the armpits,
with his own hands. She wrought so, in his burial   440
to make his death a burden
beyond your strength to carry.
The mutilation of your father. Hear it.

Electra
You tell of how my father was murdered. Meanwhile I   445
stood apart, dishonored, nothing worth,
in the dark corner, as you would kennel a vicious dog,
and burst in an outrush of tears, that came that day
where smiles would not, and hid the streaming of my
     grief.
Hear such, and carve the letters of it on your heart.   450

Chorus
Let words such as these
drip deep in your ears, but on a quiet heart.
So far all stands as it stands;

what is to come, yourself burn to know.
You must be hard, give no ground, to win home.   455

Orestes
I speak to you. Be with those you love, my father.

Electra
And I, all in my tears, ask with him.

Chorus
We gather into murmurous revolt. Hear
us, hear. Come back into the light.
Be with us against those we hate.   460

Orestes
Warstrength shall collide with warstrength; right
    with right.

Electra
O gods, be just in what you bring to pass.

Chorus
My flesh crawls as I listen to them pray.
The day of doom has waited long.
They call for it. It may come.   465

O pain grown into the race
and blood-dripping stroke
and grinding cry of disaster,
moaning and impossible weight to bear.
Sickness that fights all remedy.   470

Here in the house there lies
the cure for this, not to be brought
from outside, never from others
but in themselves, through the fierce wreck and
    bloodshed.
Here is a song sung to the gods beneath us.   475
Hear then, you blessed ones under the ground,
and answer these prayers with strength on our side,
free gift for your children's conquest.

Orestes

Father, o King who died no kingly death, I ask
the gift of lordship at your hands, to rule your house.   480

Electra

I too, my father, ask of you such grace as this:
to murder Aegisthus with strong hand, and then go free.

Orestes

So shall your memory have the feasts that men honor
in custom. Otherwise when feasts are gay, and por-
    tions
burn for the earth, you shall be there, and none
    give heed.   485

Electra

I too out of my own full dowership shall bring
libations for my bridal from my father's house.
Of all tombs, yours shall be the lordliest in my eyes.

Orestes

O Earth, let my father emerge to watch me fight.

Electra

Persephone, grant still the wonder of success.   490

Orestes

Think of that bath, father, where you were stripped
    of life.

Electra

Think of the casting net that they contrived for you.

Orestes

They caught you like a beast in toils no bronzesmith
    made.

Electra

Rather, hid you in shrouds that were thought out in
    shame.

Orestes

Will you not waken, father, to these challenges?   495

Electra
Will you not rear upright that best beloved head?

Orestes
Send out your right to battle on the side of those
you love, or give us holds like those they caught
    you in.
For they threw you. Would you not see them thrown
    in turn?

Electra
Hear one more cry, father, from me. It is my last.   500
Your nestlings huddle suppliant at your tomb: look
    forth
and pity them, female with the male strain alike.
Do not wipe out this seed of the Pelopidae.
So, though you died, you shall not yet be dead, for
    when
a man dies, children are the voice of his salvation   505
afterward. Like corks upon the net, these hold
the drenched and flaxen meshes, and they will not
    drown.
Hear us, then. Our complaints are for your sake,
    and if
you honor this our argument, you save yourself.

Chorus
None can find fault with the length of this discourse
    you drew   510
out, to show honor to a grave and fate unwept
before. The rest is action. Since your heart is set
that way, now you must strike and prove your
    destiny.

Orestes
So. But I am not wandering from my strict course
when I ask why she sent these libations, for what
    cause   515
she acknowledges, too late, a crime for which there is

122

no cure. Here was a wretched grace brought to a
  man
dead and unfeeling. This I fail to understand.
The offerings are too small for the act done. Pour out
all your possessions to atone one act of blood,   520
you waste your work, it is all useless, reason says.
Explain me this, for I would learn it, if you know.

Chorus

I know, child, I was there. It was the dreams she
  had.
The godless woman had been shaken in the night
by floating terrors, when she sent these offerings.   525

Orestes

Do you know the dream, too? Can you tell it to me
  right?

Chorus

She told me herself. She dreamed she gave birth to a
  snake.

Orestes

What is the end of the story then? What is the point?

Chorus

She laid it swathed for sleep as if it were a child.

Orestes

A little monster. Did it want some kind of food?   530

Chorus

She herself, in the dream, gave it her breast to suck.

Orestes

How was her nipple not torn by such a beastly thing?

Chorus

It was. The creature drew in blood along with the
  milk.

Orestes

No void dream this. It is the vision of a man.

Chorus

She woke screaming out of her sleep, shaky with
    fear,   535
as torches kindled all about the house, out of
the blind dark that had been on them, to comfort
    the queen.
So now she sends these mourning offerings to be
    poured
and hopes they are medicinal for her disease.

Orestes

But I pray to the earth and to my father's grave   540
that this dream is for me and that I will succeed.
See, I divine it, and it coheres all in one piece.
If this snake came out of the same place whence I
    came,
if she wrapped it in robes, as she wrapped me, and if
its jaws gaped wide around the breast that suckled
    me,   545
and if it stained the intimate milk with an outburst
of blood, so that for fright and pain she cried aloud,
it follows then, that as she nursed this hideous thing
of prophecy, she must be cruelly murdered. I
turn snake to kill her. This is what the dream por-
    tends.   550

Chorus

I choose you my interpreter to read these dreams.
So may it happen. Now you must rehearse your side
in their parts. For some, this means the parts they
    must not play.

Orestes

Simple to tell them. My sister here must go inside.
I charge her to keep secret what we have agreed,   555
so that, as they by treachery killed a man of high
degree, by treachery tangled in the self-same net
they too shall die, in the way Loxias has ordained,
my lord Apollo, whose word was never false before.

Disguised as an outlander, for which I have all gear,⁣ 560
I shall go to the outer gates with Pylades
whom you see here. He is hereditary friend
and companion-in-arms of my house. We two shall
both assume
the Parnassian dialect and imitate the way
they talk in Phocis. If none at the door will take us
in 565
kindly, because the house is in a curse of ills,
we shall stay there, till anybody who goes by
the house will wonder why we are shut out, and say:
"why does Aegisthus keep the suppliant turned away
from his gates, if he is hereabouts and knows of
this?" 570
But if I once cross the doorstone of the outer gates
and find my man seated upon my father's throne,
or if he comes down to confront me, and uplifts
his eyes to mine, then lets them drop again, be sure,
before he can say: "where does the stranger come
from?" I 575
shall plunge my sword with lightning speed, and drop
him dead.
Our Fury who is never starved for blood shall drink
for the third time a cupful of unwatered blood.

Electra, keep a careful eye on all within
the house, so that our plans will hold together. You, 580
women: I charge you, hold your tongues religiously.
Be silent if you must, or speak in the way that will
help us. And now I call upon the god who stands
close, to look on, and guide the actions of my sword.

*(Exeunt Orestes and Pylades.
Exit separately, Electra.)*

Chorus
Numberless, the earth breeds 585
dangers, and the sober thought of fear.
The bending sea's arms swarm
with bitter, savage beasts.

Torches blossom to burn along
the high space between ground and sky.   590
Things fly, and things walk the earth.
Remember too
the storm and wrath of the whirlwind.

But who can recount all
the high daring in the will   595
of man, and in the stubborn hearts of women
the all-adventurous passions
that couple with man's overthrow.
The female force, the desperate
love crams its resisted way   600
on marriage and the dark embrace
of brute beasts, of mortal men.

Let him, who goes not on flimsy wings
of thought, learn from her,
Althaea, Thestius'
daughter: who maimed her child, and hard   605
of heart, in deliberate guile
set fire to the bloody torch, her own son's
agemate, that from the day he emerged
from the mother's womb crying
shared the measure of all his life   610
down to the marked death day.

And in the legends there is one more, a girl
of blood, figure of hate
who, for the enemy's   615
sake killed one near in blood, seduced by the wrought
golden necklace from Crete,
wherewith Minos bribed her. She sundered
from Nisus his immortal hair
as he all unsuspecting   620
breathed in a tranquil sleep. Foul wretch,
Hermes of death has got her now.

Since I recall cruelties from quarrels long
ago, in vain, and married love turned to bitterness

a house would fend far away   625
by curse; the guile, treacheries of the woman's heart
against a lord armored in
power, a lord his enemies revered,
I prize the hearth not inflamed within the house,
the woman's right pushed not into daring.   630

Of all foul things legends tell the Lemnian
outranks, a vile wizard's charm, detestable
so that man names a hideous
crime "Lemnian" in memory of their wickedness.
When once the gods loathe a breed   635
of men they go outcast and forgotten.
No man respects what the gods have turned against.
What of these tales I gather has no meaning?

The sword edges near the lungs.
It stabs deep, bittersharp,   640
and right drives it. For that which had no right
lies not yet stamped into the ground, although
one in sin transgressed Zeus' majesty.   645

Right's anvil stands staunch on the ground
and the smith, Destiny, hammers out the sword.
Delayed in glory, pensive from
the murk, Vengeance brings home at last   650
a child, to wipe out the stain of blood shed long ago.

(Enter Orestes and Pylades.)

Orestes

In there! Inside! Does anyone hear me knocking at
the gate? I will try again. Is anyone at home?
Try a third time. I ask for someone to come from the
  house,   655
if Aegisthus lets it welcome friendly visitors.

Servant (inside)

All right, I hear you. Where does the stranger come
  from, then?

Orestes

Announce me to the masters of the house. It is
to them I come, and I have news for them to hear.
And be quick, for the darkening chariot of night   660
leans to its course; the hour for wayfarers to drop
anchor in some place that entertains all travelers.
Have someone of authority in the house come out,
the lady of the place or, more appropriately,
its lord, for then no delicacy in speaking blurs   665
the spoken word. A man takes courage and speaks
out
to another man, and makes clear everything he
means.

(*Enter Clytaemestra.*)

Clytaemestra

Friends, tell me only what you would have, and it is
yours.
We have all comforts that go with a house like ours,
hot baths, and beds to charm away your weariness   670
with rest, and the regard of temperate eyes. But if
you have some higher business, more a matter of
state,
that is the men's concern, and I will tell them of it.

Orestes

I am a Daulian stranger out of Phocis. As
I traveled with my pack and my own following   675
making for Argos, where my feet are rested now,
I met a man I did not know, nor did he know
me, but he asked what way I took, and told me his.
It was a Phocian, Strophius; for he told me his name
and said: "Friend, since in any case you make for
Argos,   680
remember carefully to tell Orestes' parents
that he is dead; please do not let it slip your mind.
Then, if his people decide to have him brought back
home,

or bury him where he went to live, all outlander
forever, carry their requests again to me.   685
For as it is the bronze walls of an urn close in
the ashes of a man who has been deeply mourned."

So much I know, no more. But whether I now talk
with those who have authority and concern in this
I do not know. I think his father should be told.   690

Clytaemestra

Ah me. You tell us how we are stormed from head to
    heel.
Oh curse upon our house, bitter antagonist,
how far your eyes range. What was clean out of your
    way
your archery brings down with a distant deadly shot
to strip unhappy me of all I ever loved.   695
Even Orestes now! He was so well advised
to keep his foot clear of this swamp of death. But
    now
set down as traitor the hope that was our healer once
and made us look for a bright revel in our house.

Orestes

I could have wished, with hosts so prosperous as you,   700
to have made myself known by some more gracious
    news
and so been entertained by you. For what is there
more kindly than the feeling between host and guest?
Yet it had been abuse of duty in my heart
had I not given so great a matter to his friends,   705
being so bound by promise and the stranger's rights.

Clytaemestra

You shall not find that your reception falls below
your worth, nor be any the less our friend for this.
Some other would have brought the news in any
    case.
But it is the hour for travelers who all day have
    trudged   710

the long road, to be given the rest that they deserve.
Escort this gentleman with his companion and
his men, to where our masculine friends are made
    at home.
Look after them, in manner worthy of a house
like ours; you are responsible for their good care.   715
Meanwhile, we shall communicate these matters to
the masters of the house, and with our numerous
    friends
deliberate the issues of this fatal news.

                        (*Exeunt all but the Chorus.*)

Chorus
Handmaidens of this house, who help our cause,
how can our lips frame   720
some force that will show for Orestes?
O Lady Earth, Earth Queen, who now
ride mounded over the lord of ships
where the King's corpse lies buried,
hear us, help us.   725
Now the time breaks for Persuasion in stealth
to go down to the pit, with Hermes of death
and the dark, to direct
trial by the sword's fierce edge.

I think our newcomer is at his deadly work;   730
I see Orestes' old nurse coming forth, in tears.

                                    (*Enter Cilissa.*)

Now where away, Cilissa, through the castle gates,
with sorrow as your hireless fellow-wayfarer?

Cilissa
The woman who is our mistress told me to make
    haste
and summon Aegisthus for the strangers, "so that he   735
can come and hear, as man to man, in more detail
this news that they have brought." She put a sad
    face on

130

before the servants, to hide the smile inside her eyes
over this work that has been done so happily
for her—though on this house the curse is now com-
plete   740
from the plain story that the stranger men have
    brought.
But as for that Aegisthus, oh, he will be pleased
enough to hear the story. Poor unhappy me,
all my long-standing mixture of misfortunes, hard
burden enough, here in this house of Atreus,   745
when it befell me made the heart ache in my breast.
But never yet did I have to bear a hurt like this.
I took the other troubles bravely as they came:
but now, darling Orestes! I wore out my life
for him. I took him from his mother, brought him up.   750
There were times when he screamed at night and
    woke me from
my rest; I had to do many hard tasks, and now
useless; a baby is like a beast, it does not think
but you have to nurse it, do you not, the way it
    wants.
For the child still in swaddling clothes can not tell us   755
if he is hungry or thirsty, if he needs to make
water. Children's young insides are a law to them-
    selves.
I needed second sight for this, and many a time
I think I missed, and had to wash the baby's clothes.
The nurse and laundrywoman had a combined duty   760
and that was I. I was skilled in both handicrafts,
and so Orestes' father gave him to my charge.
And now, unhappy, I am told that he is dead
and go to take the story to that man who has
defiled our house; he will be glad to hear such news.   765

Chorus
Did she say he should come back armed in any way?

Cilissa
How, armed? Say it again. I do not understand.

Chorus
Was he to come with bodyguards, or by himself?

Cilissa
She said to bring his followers, the men-at-arms.

Chorus
Now, if you hate our master, do not tell him that,   770
but simply bid him come as quickly as he can
and cheerfully. In that way he will not take fright.
It is the messenger who makes the bent word
    straight.

Cilissa
But are you happy over what I have told you?

Chorus
Perhaps: if Zeus might turn our evil wind to good.   775

Cilissa
How so? Orestes, once hope of the house, is gone.

Chorus
Not yet. It would be a poor seer who saw it thus.

Cilissa
What is this? Have you some news that has not been
    told?

Chorus
Go on and take your message, do as you were bid.
The gods' concerns are what concern only the gods.   780

Cilissa
I will go then and do all this as you have told
me to. May all be for the best. So grant us god.

                                    (*Exit Cilissa.*)

Chorus
Now to my supplication, Zeus,
father of Olympian gods,
grant that those who struggle hard to see   785

temperate things done in the house win their aim
in full. All that I spoke
was spoken in right. Yours, Zeus, to protect.

Zeus, Zeus, make him who is now
in the house stand above those who   790
hate. If you rear him to greatness,
double and three times
and blithely he will repay you.

See the colt of this man whom you loved
harnessed to the chariot   795
of suffering. Set upon the race he runs
sure control. Make us not see him break
stride, but clean down the course
hold the strain of his striding speed.

You that, deep in the house   800
sway their secret pride of wealth,
hear us, gods of sympathy.
For things done in time past
wash out the blood in fair-spoken verdict.
Let the old murder in   805
the house breed no more.

And you, who keep, magnificent, the hallowed and
     huge
cavern, o grant that the man's house lift up its head
and look on the shining of daylight
and liberty with eyes made
glad with gazing out from the helm of darkness.   810

And with right may the son
of Maia lend his hand, strong to send
wind fair for action, if he will.
Much else lies secret he may show at need.   815
He speaks the markless word, by
night hoods darkness on the eyes
nor shows more plainly when the day is there.
Then at last we shall sing

for deliverance of the house   820
the woman's song that sets the wind
fair, no thin drawn and grief
struck wail, but this: "The ship sails fair."
My way, mine, the advantage piles here, with wreck
and ruin far from those I love.   825

Be not fear struck when your turn comes in the
    action
but with a great cry *Father*
when she cries *Child* to you
go on through with the innocent murder.   830

Yours to raise high within
your body the heart of Perseus
and for those under the ground you loved
and those yet above, exact
what their bitter passion may desire; make   835
disaster a thing of blood inside the house;
wipe out the man stained with murder.

                        (*Enter Aegisthus.*)

Aegisthus
It is not without summons that I come, but called
by messenger, with news that there are strangers here
arrived, telling a story that brings no delight: 840
the death of Orestes. For our house, already bitten
and poisoned, to take this new load upon itself
would be a thing of dripping fear and blood. Yet how
shall I pass upon these rumors? As the living truth?
For messages made out of women's terror leap   845
high in the upward air and empty die. Do *you*
know anything of this by which to clear my mind?

Chorus
We heard, yes. But go on inside and hear it from
the strangers. Messengers are never quite so sure
as a man's questions answered by the men them-
    selves.   850

134

Aegisthus
I wish to question, carefully, this messenger
and learn if he himself was by when the man died
or if he heard but some blind rumor and so speaks.
The mind has eyes, not to be easily deceived.

(*Exit Aegisthus.*)

Chorus
Zeus, Zeus, what shall I say, where make   855
a beginning of prayer for the gods' aid?
My will is good
but how shall I speak to match my need?
The bloody edges of the knives that rip
man-flesh are moving to work. It will mean   860
utter and final ruin imposed
on Agamemnon's
house: or our man will kindle a flame
and light of liberty, win the domain
and huge treasure again of his fathers.   865
Forlorn challenger, though blessed by god,
Orestes must come to grips with two,
so wrestle. Yet may he throw them.

(*A cry is heard from inside the house.*)

Listen, it goes   870
but how? What has been done in the house?
Stand we aside until the work is done, for so
we shall not seem to be accountable in this
foul business. For the fight is done, the issue drawn.

(*Enter a follower of Aegisthus.*)

Follower
O sorrow, all is sorrow for our stricken lord.   875
Raise up again a triple cry of sorrow, for
Aegisthus lives no longer. Open there, open
quick as you may, and slide back the doorbars on the
    women's

gates. It will take the strength of a young arm, but
  not
to fight for one who is dead and done for. What use   880
  there?
Ahoy!
My cry is to the deaf and I babble in vain
at sleepers to no purpose. Clytaemestra, where
is she, does what? Her neck is on the razor's edge
and ripe for lopping, as she did to others before.

(*Enter Clytaemestra.*)

Clytaemestra
What is this, and why are you shouting in the house?   885

Follower
I tell you, he is alive and killing the dead.

Clytaemestra
Ah, so. You speak in riddles, but I read the rhyme.
We have been won with the treachery by which we
  slew.
Bring me quick, somebody, an ax to kill a man

(*Exit follower.*)

and we shall see if we can beat him before we   890
go down—so far gone are we in this wretched fight.

(*Enter Orestes and Pylades with swords drawn.*)

Orestes
You next: the other one in there has had enough.

Clytaemestra
Beloved, strong Aegisthus, are you dead indeed?

Orestes
You love your man, then? You shall lie in the same
  grave
with him, and never be unfaithful even in death.   895

Clytaemestra
Hold, my son. Oh take pity, child, before this breast

136

where many a time, a drowsing baby, you would
  feed
and with soft gums sucked in the milk that made
  you strong.

Orestes

What shall I do, Pylades? Be shamed to kill my
  mother?

Pylades

What then becomes thereafter of the oracles   900
declared by Loxias at Pytho? What of sworn oaths?
Count all men hateful to you rather than the gods.

Orestes

I judge that you win. Your advice is good.

(*To Clytaemestra.*)

Come here.
My purpose is to kill you over his body.
You thought him bigger than my father while he
  lived.   905
Die then and sleep beside him, since he is the man
you love, and he you should have loved got only your
  hate.

Clytaemestra

I raised you when you were little. May I grow old
  with you?

Orestes

You killed my father. Would you make your home
  with me?

Clytaemestra

Destiny had some part in that, my child.

Orestes

Why then   910
destiny has so wrought that this shall be your death.

Clytaemestra
A mother has her curse, child. Are you not afraid?

Orestes
No. You bore me and threw me away, to a hard life.

Clytaemestra
I sent you to a friend's house. This was no throwing away.

Orestes
I was born of a free father. You sold me.   915

Clytaemestra
So? Where then is the price that I received for you?

Orestes
I could say. It would be indecent to tell you.

Clytaemestra
Or if you do, tell also your father's vanities.

Orestes
Blame him not. He suffered while you were sitting here at home.

Clytaemestra
It hurts women to be kept from their men, my child.   920

Orestes
The man's hard work supports the women who sit at home.

Clytaemestra
I think, child, that you mean to kill your mother.

Orestes
                                              No.
It will be you who kill yourself. It will not be I.

Clytaemestra
Take care. Your mother's curse, like dogs, will drag you down.

138

Orestes
How shall I escape my father's curse, if I fail here?   925

Clytaemestra
I feel like one who wastes live tears upon a tomb.

Orestes
Yes, this is death, your wages for my father's fate.

Clytaemestra
You are the snake I gave birth to, and gave the breast.

Orestes
Indeed, the terror of your dreams saw things to come
clearly. You killed, and it was wrong. Now suffer
wrong.   930

> (*Orestes and Pylades take Clytaemestra*
>   *inside the house.*)

Chorus
I have sorrow even for this pair in their twofold
downfall. But since Orestes had the hardiness
to end this chain of bloodlettings, here lies our
    choice,
that the eyes' light in this house shall not utterly die.

Justice came at the last to Priam and all his sons   935
and it was heavy and hard,
but into the house of Agamemnon returned
the double lion, the double assault,
and the Pythian-steered exile
drove home to the hilt   940
vengeance, moving strongly in guidance sent by the
    god.

Raise up the high cry o over our lordships' house
won free of distress, free of its fortunes wasted
by two stained with murder,
free of its mournful luck.   945

He came back; his work lay in the secret attack
and it was stealthy and hard
but in the fighting his hand was steered by the very
    daughter
of Zeus: Right we call her,
mortals who speak of her and name her well. Her
    wind   950
is fury and death visited upon those she hates.

All that Loxias, who on Parnassus holds
the huge, the deep cleft in the ground, shrilled aloud,
by guile that is no guile   955
returns now to assault the wrong done and grown
    old.
Divinity keeps, we know not how, strength to resist
surrender to the wicked.
The power that holds the sky's majesty wins our
    worship.   960

Light is here to behold.
The big bit that held our house is taken away.
Rise up, you halls, arise; for time grown too long
you lay tumbled along the ground.
Time brings all things to pass. Presently time shall
    cross   965
the outgates of the house after the stain is driven
entire from the hearth
by ceremonies that wash clean and cast out the
    furies.
The dice of fortune shall be thrown once more, and
    lie
in a fair fall smiling   970
up at the new indwellers come to live in the house.

(*The doors of the house open, to show Orestes standing over the bodies of Clytaemestra and Aegisthus.
His attendants display the robe in which Clytaemestra had entangled Agamemnon and which
she displayed after his murder.*)

Orestes
Behold the twin tyrannies of our land, these two
who killed my father and who sacked my house. For
  a time
they sat upon their thrones and kept their pride of
  state,   975
and they are lovers still. So may you judge by what
befell them, for as they were pledged their oath
  abides.
They swore together death for my unhappy sire
and swore to die together. Now they keep their oath.

Behold again, o audience of these evil things,   980
the engine against my wretched father they devised,
the hands' entanglement, the hobbles for his feet.
Spread it out. Stand around me in a circle and
display this net that caught a man. So shall, not my
father, but that great father who sees all, the Sun,   985
look on my mother's sacrilegious handiwork
and be a witness for me in my day of trial
how it was in all right that I achieved this death,
my mother's: for of Aegisthus' death I take no count:
he has his seducer's punishment, no more than law.   990

But she, who plotted this foul death against the man
by whom she carried the weight of children underneath
her zone, burden once loved, shown hard and hateful
  now,
what does she seem to be? Some water snake, some
  viper
whose touch is rot even to him who felt no fang   995
strike, by that brutal and wrong daring in her heart.

And this thing: what shall I call it and be right, in all
eloquence? Trap for an animal or winding sheet
for dead man? Or bath curtain? Since it is a net,
robe you could call it, to entangle a man's feet.   1000

141

Some highwayman might own a thing like this, to catch
the wayfarer and rob him of his money and
so make a living. With a treacherous thing like this
he could take many victims and go warm within.

May no such wife as she was come to live with me.   1005
Sooner, let God destroy me, with no children born.

Chorus
Ah, but the pitiful work.
Dismal the death that was your ending.
He is left alive; pain flowers for him.

Orestes
Did she do it or did she not? My witness is   1010
this great robe. It was thus she stained Aegisthus'
    sword.
Dip it and dip it again, the smear of blood conspires
with time to spoil the beauty of this precious thing.
Now I can praise him, now I can stand by to mourn
and speak before this web that killed my father; yet   1015
I grieve for the thing done, the death, and all
    our race.
I have won; but my victory is soiled, and has no pride.

Chorus
There is no mortal man who shall turn
unhurt his life's course to an end not marred.
There is trouble here. There is more to come.   1020

Orestes
I would have you know, I see not how this thing
    will end.
I am a charioteer whose course is wrenched outside
the track, for I am beaten, my rebellious senses
bolt with me headlong and the fear against my heart
is ready for the singing and dance of wrath. But while   1025
I hold some grip still on my wits, I say publicly

to my friends: I killed my mother not without some
   right.
My father's murder stained her, and the gods' disgust.
As for the spells that charmed me to such daring, I
give you in chief the seer of Pytho, Loxias. He   1030
declared I could do this and not be charged with
   wrong.
Of my evasion's punishment I will not speak:
no archery could hit such height of agony.
And look upon me now, how I go armored in
leafed branch and garland on my way to the centrestone   1035
and sanctuary, and Apollo's level place,
the shining of the fabulous fire that never dies,
to escape this blood that is my own. Loxias ordained
that I should turn me to no other shrine than this.
To all men of Argos in time to come I say   1040
they shall be witness, how these evil things were done.
I go, an outcast wanderer from this land, and leave
behind, in life, in death, the name of what I did.

Chorus
No, what you did was well done. Do not therefore bind
your mouth to foul speech. Keep no evil on your lips.   1045
You liberated all the Argive city when
you lopped the heads of these two snakes with one
   clean stroke.

Orestes
No!
Women who serve this house, they come like gorgons,
   they
wear robes of black, and they are wreathed in a tangle
of snakes. I can no longer stay.   1050

Chorus
Orestes, dearest to your father of all men
what fancies whirl you? Hold, do not give way to fear.

Orestes
These are no fancies of affliction. They are clear,
and real, and here; the bloodhounds of my mother's
    hate.

Chorus
It is the blood still wet upon your hands, that makes   1055
this shaken turbulence be thrown upon your sense.

Orestes
Ah, Lord Apollo, how they grow and multiply,
repulsive for the blood drops of their dripping eyes.

Chorus
There is one way to make you clean: let Loxias
touch you, and set you free from these disturbances.   1060

Orestes
You can not see them, but I see them. I am driven
from this place. I can stay here no longer.

                                                    (*Exit.*)

Chorus
Good luck go with you then, and may the god look on
you with favor and guard you in kind circumstance.

Here on this house of the kings the third   1065
storm has broken, with wind
from the inward race, and gone its course.
The children were eaten: there was the first
affliction, the curse of Thyestes.
Next came the royal death, when a man   1070
and lord of Achaean armies went down
killed in the bath. Third
is for the savior. He came. Shall I call
it that, or death? Where
is the end? Where shall the fury of fate   1075
be stilled to sleep, be done with?

                                                    (*Exeunt.*)

THE EUMENIDES

CHARACTERS

Priestess of Apollo, the Pythia

Apollo

Hermes (silent)

Ghost of Clytaemestra

Orestes

Athene

Chorus of Eumenides (Furies)

Second Chorus; women of Athens

Jurymen, herald, citizens of Athens (all silent parts)

146

THE EUMENIDES

SCENE: *For the first part of the play (1–234) the scene is Delphi, before the sanctuary of Pythian Apollo. The action of the rest of the play (235 to the end) takes place at Athens, on the Acropolis before the temple of Athene. A simple change in the backdrop will indicate the shift.*

(Enter, alone, the Pythia.)

Pythia
I give first place of honor in my prayer to her
who of the gods first prophesied, the Earth; and next
to Themis, who succeeded to her mother's place
of prophecy; so runs the legend; and in third
succession, given by free consent, not won by force,   5
another Titan daughter of Earth was seated here.
This was Phoebe. She gave it as a birthday gift
to Phoebus, who is called still after Phoebe's name.
And he, leaving the pond of Delos and the reef,
grounded his ship at the roadstead of Pallas, then   10
made his way to this land and a Parnassian home.
Deep in respect for his degree Hephaestus' sons
conveyed him here, for these are builders of roads,
   and changed
the wilderness to a land that was no wilderness.
He came so, and the people highly honored him,   15
with Delphus, lord and helmsman of the country.
   Zeus
made his mind full with godship and prophetic craft
and placed him, fourth in a line of seers, upon this
   throne.

147

So, Loxias is the spokesman of his father, Zeus.
    These are the gods I set in the proem of my prayer.   20
But Pallas-before-the-temple has her right in all
I say. I worship the nymphs where the Corycian rock
is hollowed inward, haunt of birds and paced by gods.
Bromius, whom I forget not, sways this place.
  From here
in divine form he led his Bacchanals in arms   25
to hunt down Pentheus like a hare in the deathtrap.
I call upon the springs of Pleistus, on the power
of Poseidon, and on final loftiest Zeus,
then go to sit in prophecy on the throne. May all
grant me that this of all my entrances shall be   30
the best by far. If there are any Hellenes here
let them draw lots, so enter, as the custom is.
My prophecy is only as the god may guide.

      (She enters the temple and almost immediately
                  comes out again.)

Things terrible to tell and for the eyes to see
terrible drove me out again from Loxias' house   35
so that I have no strength and can not stand on
  springing
feet, but run with hands' help and my legs have
  no speed.
An old woman afraid is nothing: a child, no more.
  See, I am on my way to the wreath-hung recess
and on the centrestone I see a man with god's   40
defilement on him postured in the suppliant's seat
with blood dripping from his hands and from a new-
  drawn sword,
holding too a branch that had grown high on an olive
tree, decorously wrapped in a great tuft of wool,
and the fleece shone. So far, at least, I can speak clear.   45
  In front of this man slept a startling company
of women lying all upon the chairs. Or not
women, I think I call them rather gorgons, only
not gorgons either, since their shape is not the same.

I saw some creatures painted in a picture once,   50
who tore the food from Phineus, only these had no
wings, that could be seen; they are black and utterly
repulsive, and they snore with breath that drives
   one back.
From their eyes drips the foul ooze, and their dress
   is such
as is not right to wear in the presence of the gods'   55
statues, nor even into any human house.
I have never seen the tribe that owns this company
nor know what piece of earth can claim with pride
   it bore
such brood, and without hurt and tears for labor given.
   Now after this the master of the house must take   60
his own measures: Apollo Loxias, who is very strong
and heals by divination; reads portentous signs,
and so clears out the houses others hold as well.

   (*Exit. The doors of the temple open and show*
         Orestes surrounded by the sleeping Furies,
                  Apollo and Hermes beside him.)

Apollo
I will not give you up. Through to the end standing
your guardian, whether by your side or far away,   65
I shall not weaken toward your enemies. See now
how I have caught and overpowered these lewd
   creatures.
The repulsive maidens have been stilled to sleep,
   those gray
and aged children, they with whom no mortal man,
no god, nor even any beast, will have to do.   70
It was because of evil they were born, because
they hold the evil darkness of the Pit below
Earth, loathed alike by men and by the heavenly gods.
Nevertheless, run from them, never weaken. They
will track you down as you stride on across the long   75
land, and your driven feet forever pound the earth,
on across the main water and the circle-washed

cities. Be herdsman to this hard march. Never fail
until you come at last to Pallas' citadel.
Kneel there, and clasp the ancient idol in your arms,   80
and there we shall find those who will judge this
      case, and words
to say that will have magic in their figures. Thus
you will be rid of your afflictions, once for all.
For it was I who made you strike your mother down.

Orestes
My lord Apollo, you understand what it means to do   85
no wrong. Learn also what it is not to neglect.
None can mistrust your power to do good, if you will.

Apollo
Remember: the fear must not give you a beaten heart.
Hermes, you are my brother from a single sire.
Look after him, and as you are named the god who
      guides,   90
be such in strong fact. He is my suppliant. Shepherd
      him
with fortunate escort on his journeys among men.
The wanderer has rights which Zeus acknowledges.

(*Exit Apollo, then Orestes guided by Hermes. Enter
      the ghost of Clytaemestra.*)

Clytaemestra
You would sleep, then? And what use are you, if
      you sleep?
It is because of you I go dishonored thus   95
among the rest of the dead. Because of those I killed
my bad name among the perished suffers no eclipse
but I am driven in disgrace. I say to you
that I am charged with guilt most grave by these.
      And yet
I suffered too, horribly, and from those most dear,   100
yet none among the powers is angered for my sake
that I was slaughtered, and by matricidal hands.

Look at these gashes in my heart, think where they
    came
from. Eyes illuminate the sleeping brain,
but in the daylight man's future cannot be seen.   105
    Yet I have given you much to lap up, outpourings
without wine, sober propitiations, sacrificed
in secrecy of night and on a hearth of fire
for you, at an hour given to no other god.
Now I watch all these honors trampled into the
    ground,   110
and he is out and gone away like any fawn
so lightly, from the very middle of your nets,
sprung clear, and laughing merrily at you. Hear me.
It is my life depends upon this spoken plea.
Think then, o goddesses beneath the ground. For I,   115
the dream of Clytaemestra, call upon your name.

            (*The Furies stir in their sleep and whimper.*)

Clytaemestra
Oh, whimper, then, but your man has got away
    and gone
far. He has friends to help him, who are not like mine.

                    (*They whimper again.*)   120

Clytaemestra
Too much sleep and no pity for my plight. I stand,
his mother, here, killed by Orestes. He is gone.

                    (*They moan in their sleep.*)

Clytaemestra
You moan, you sleep. Get on your feet quickly,
    will you?
What have you yet got done, except to do evil?   125

                    (*They moan again.*)

Clytaemestra
Sleep and fatigue, two masterful conspirators,
have dimmed the deadly anger of the mother-snake.

*(The Chorus start violently, then speak
in their sleep.)*

Chorus
Get him, get him, get him, get him. Make sure.　　130

Clytaemestra
The beast you are after is a dream, but like the hound
whose thought of hunting has no lapse, you bay
 him on.
What are you about? Up, let not work's weariness
beat you, nor slacken with sleep so you forget my pain.
Scold your own heart and hurt it, as it well deserves,　135
for this is discipline's spur upon her own. Let go
upon this man the stormblasts of your bloodshot
 breath,
wither him in your wind, after him, hunt him down
once more, and shrivel him in your vitals' heat and
 flame.

*(The ghost disappears, and the Chorus waken and,
as they waken, speak severally.)*

Chorus
Waken. You are awake, wake her, as I did you.　　140
You dream still? On your feet and kick your sleep
 aside.
Let us see whether this morning-song means vanity.

(Here they begin to howl.)

Sisters, we have had wrong done us.
When I have undergone so much and all in vain.
Suffering, suffering, bitter, oh shame shame,　　145
unendurable wrong.
The hunted beast has slipped clean from our nets
 and gone.
Sleep won me, and I lost my capture.

Shame, son of Zeus! Robber is all you are.
A young god, you have ridden down powers gray
 with age,　　150

taken the suppliant, though a godless man, who hurt
the mother who gave him birth.
Yourself a god, you stole the matricide away.
Where in this act shall any man say there is right?

The accusation came upon me from my dreams,   155
and hit me, as with goad in the mid-grip of his fist
the charioteer strikes,
but deep, beneath lobe and heart.
The executioner's cutting whip is mine to feel   160
and the weight of pain is big, heavy to bear.

Such are the actions of the younger gods. These hold
by unconditional force, beyond all right, a throne
that runs reeking blood,
blood at the feet, blood at the head.   165
The very stone centre of earth here in our eyes horrible
with blood and curse stands plain to see.

Himself divine, he has spoiled his secret shrine's
hearth with the stain, driven and hallooed the action
   on.   170
He made man's way cross the place of the ways of god
and blighted age-old distributions of power.
He has wounded me, but he shall not get this man
   away.
Let him hide under the ground, he shall never go free.   175
Cursed suppliant, he shall feel against his head
another murderer rising out of the same seed.

(*Apollo enters again from his sanctuary.*)

Apollo
Get out, I tell you, go and leave this house. Away
in haste, from your presence set the mantic chamber
   free,   180
else you may feel the flash and bite of a flying snake
launched from the twisted thong of gold that spans
   my bow

to make you in your pain spew out the black and
    foaming
blood of men, vomit the clots sucked from their veins.
This house is no right place for such as you to cling   185
upon; but where, by judgment given, heads are lopped
and eyes gouged out, throats cut, and by the spoil
    of sex
the glory of young boys is defeated, where mutilation
lives, and stoning, and the long moan of tortured men
spiked underneath the spine and stuck on pales. Listen   190
to how the gods spit out the manner of that feast
your loves lean to. The whole cast of your shape
    is guide
to what you are, the like of whom should hole in
    the cave
of the blood-reeking lion, not in oracular
interiors, like mine nearby, wipe off your filth.   195
Out then, you flock of goats without a herdsman,
    since
no god has such affection as to tend this brood.

Chorus
My lord Apollo, it is your turn to listen now.
Your own part in this is more than accessory.
You are the one who did it; all the guilt is yours.   200

Apollo
So? How? Continue speaking, until I understand.

Chorus
You gave this outlander the word to kill his mother.

Apollo
The word to exact price for his father. What of that?

Chorus
You then dared take him in, fresh from his blood-
    letting.

Apollo
Yes, and I told him to take refuge in this house.   205

Chorus
You are abusive then to those who sped him here?

Apollo
Yes. It was not for you to come near this house;

Chorus
                                                    and yet
we have our duty. It was to do what we have done.

Apollo
An office? You? Sound forth your glorious privilege.

Chorus
This: to drive matricides out of their houses.   210

Apollo
                                                    Then
what if it be the woman and she kills her man?

Chorus
Such murder would not be the shedding of kindred
    blood.

Apollo
You have made into a thing of no account, no place,
the sworn faith of Zeus and of Hera, lady
of consummations, and Cypris by such argument   215
is thrown away, outlawed, and yet the sweetest things
in man's life come from her, for married love between
man and woman is bigger than oaths, guarded by right
of nature. If when such kill each other you relent
so as not to take vengeance nor eye them in wrath,   220
then I deny your manhunt of Orestes goes
with right. I see that one cause moves you to strong
    rage
but on the other clearly you are unmoved to act.
Pallas divine shall review the pleadings of this case.

Chorus
Nothing will ever make me let that man go free.   225

Apollo
Keep after him then, and make more trouble for
  yourselves.

Chorus
Do not try to dock my privilege by argument.

Apollo
I would not take your privilege if you gave it me.

Chorus
No, for you are called great beside the throne of Zeus
already, but the motherblood drives me, and I go   230
to win my right upon this man and hunt him down.

Apollo
But I shall give the suppliant help and rescue, for
if I willingly fail him who turns to me for aid,
his wrath, before gods and men, is a fearful thing.

(*They go out, separately. The scene is now Athens,
      on the Acropolis before the temple and statue
            of Athene. Orestes enters and takes suppli-
                  ant posture at the feet of the statue.*)

Orestes
My lady Athene, it is at Loxias' behest   235
I come. Then take in of your grace the wanderer
who comes, no suppliant, not unwashed of hand,
  but one
blunted at last, and worn and battered on the outland
habitations and the beaten ways of men.
Crossing the dry land and the sea alike, keeping   240
the ordinances of Apollo's oracle
I come, goddess, before your statue and your house
to keep watch here and wait the issue of my trial.

(*The Chorus enter severally, looking for Orestes.*)

Chorus
So. Here the man has left a clear trail behind; keep on,   245
keep on, as the unspeaking accuser tells us, by

whose sense, like hounds after a bleeding fawn,
    we trail
our quarry by the splash and drip of blood. And now
my lungs are blown with abundant and with weari-
    some
work, mankilling. My range has been the entire extent
of land, and, flown unwinged across the open water,   250
I am here, and give way to no ship in my pursuit.
Our man has gone to cover somewhere in this place.
The welcome smell of human blood has told me so.

Look again, look again,
search everywhere, let   255
not the matricide
steal away and escape.

                                    (*They see Orestes.*)

See there! He clings to defence
again, his arms winding the immortal goddess'
image, so tries to be quit out of our hands.   260
It shall not be. His mother's blood spilled on the
    ground
can not come back again.
It is all soaked and drained into the ground and gone.

You must give back for her blood from the living man
red blood of your body to suck, and from your own   265
I could feed, with bitter-swallowed drench,
turn your strength limp while yet you live and drag
    you down
where you must pay for the pain of the murdered
    mother,
and watch the rest of the mortals stained with violence
against god or guest   270
or hurt parents who were close and dear,
each with the pain upon him that his crime deserves.
Hades is great, Hades calls men to reckoning
there under the ground,
sees all, and cuts it deep in his recording mind.   275

Orestes

I have been beaten and been taught, I understand
the many rules of absolution, where it is right
to speak and where be silent. In this action now
speech has been ordered by my teacher, who is wise.
The stain of blood dulls now and fades upon my
    hand.   280
My blot of matricide is being washed away.
When it was fresh still, at the hearth of the god,
    Phoebus,
this was absolved and driven out by sacrifice
of swine, and the list were long if I went back to tell
of all I met who were not hurt by being with me.   285
Time in his aging overtakes all things alike.
Now it is from pure mouth and with good auspices
I call upon Athene, queen of this land, to come
and rescue me. She, without work of her spear,
    shall win
myself and all my land and all the Argive host   290
to stand her staunch companion for the rest of time.
Whether now ranging somewhere in the Libyan land
beside her father's crossing and by Triton's run
of waters she sets upright or enshrouded foot
rescuing there her friends, or on the Phlegraean flat   295
like some bold man of armies sweeps with eyes the
    scene,
let her come! She is a god and hears me far away.
So may she set me free from what is at my back.

Chorus

Neither Apollo nor Athene's strength must win
you free, save you from going down forgotten, without   300
knowing where joy lies anywhere inside your heart,
blood drained, chewed dry by the powers of death, a
    wraith, a shell.
You will not speak to answer, spew my challenge
    away?
You are consecrate to me and fattened for my feast,

and you shall feed me while you live, not cut down
   first   305
at the altar. Hear the spell I sing to bind you in.

Come then, link we our choral. Ours
to show forth the power
and terror of our music, declare
our rights of office, how we conspire   310
to steer men's lives.
We hold we are straight and just. If a man
can spread his hands and show they are clean,
no wrath of ours shall lurk for him.
Unscathed he walks through his life time.   315
But one like this man before us, with stained
hidden hands, and the guilt upon him,
shall find us beside him, as witnesses
of the truth, and we show clear in the end
to avenge the blood of the murdered.   320

Mother, o my mother night, who gave me
birth, to be a vengeance on the seeing
and the blind, hear me. For Leto's
youngling takes my right away,
stealing from my clutch the prey   325
that crouches, whose blood would wipe
at last the motherblood away.

Over the beast doomed to the fire
this is the chant, scatter of wits,
frenzy and fear, hurting the heart,   330
song of the Furies
binding brain and blighting blood
in its stringless melody.

This the purpose that the all-involving
destiny spun, to be ours and to be shaken   335
never: when mortals assume outrage
of own hand in violence,
these we dog, till one goes

under earth. Nor does death
set them altogether free.   340

Over the beast doomed to the fire
this is the chant, scatter of wits,
frenzy and fear, hurting the heart,
song of the Furies
binding brain and blighting blood   345
in its stringless melody.

When we were born such lots were assigned for our
    keeping.
So the immortals must hold hands off, nor is there   350
one who shall sit at our feasting.
For sheer white robes I have no right and no portion.

I have chosen overthrow
of houses, where the Battlegod   355
grown within strikes near and dear
down. So we swoop upon this man
here. He is strong, but we wear him down
for the blood that is still wet on him.

Here we stand in our haste to wrench from all others   360
these devisings, make the gods clear of our counsels
so that even appeal comes
not to them, since Zeus has ruled our blood dripping
    company   365
outcast, nor will deal with us.

I have chosen overthrow
of houses, where the Battlegod
grown within strikes near and dear
down. So we swoop upon this man
here. He is strong, but we wear him down
for the blood that is still wet on him.

Men's illusions in their pride under the sky melt
down, and are diminished into the ground, gone
before the onset of our black robes, pulsing   370
of our vindictive feet against them.

For with a long leap from high
above and dead drop of weight
I bring foot's force crashing down
to cut the legs from under even   375
the runner, and spill him to ruin.

He falls, and does not know in the daze of his folly.
Such in the dark of man is the mist of infection
that hovers, and moaning rumor tells how his house
  lies
under fog that glooms above.   380

For with a long leap from high
above, and dead drop of weight,
I bring foot's force crashing down
to cut the legs from under even
the runner, and spill him to ruin.

All holds. For we are strong and skilled;
we have authority; we hold
memory of evil; we are stern
nor can men's pleadings bend us. We
drive through our duties, spurned, outcast   385
from gods, driven apart to stand in light
not of the sun. So sheer with rock are ways
for those who see, as upon those whose eyes are lost.

Is there a man who does not fear
this, does not shink to hear   390
how my place has been ordained,
granted and given by destiny
and god, absolute? Privilege
primeval yet is mine, nor am I without place
though it be underneath the ground   395
and in no sunlight and in gloom that I must stand.

(*Athene enters, in full armor.*)

Athene
From far away I heard the outcry of your call.
It was beside Scamandrus. I was taking seisin

161

of land, for there the Achaean lords of war and first
fighters gave me large portion of all their spears   400
had won, the land root and stock to be mine for all
eternity, for the sons of Theseus a choice gift.
From there, sped on my weariless feet, I came,
  wingless
but in the rush and speed of the aegis fold. And now
I see upon this land a novel company   405
which, though it brings no terror to my eyes,
  brings still
wonder. Who are you? I address you all alike,
both you, the stranger kneeling at my image here,
and you, who are like no seed ever begotten, not   410
seen ever by the gods as goddesses, nor yet
stamped in the likenesses of any human form.
But no. This is the place of the just. Its rights forbid
even the innocent to speak evil of his mates.

Chorus
Daughter of Zeus, you shall hear all compressed
  to brief   415
measure. We are the gloomy children of the night.
Curses they call us in our homes beneath the ground.

Athene
I know your race, then, and the names by which you
  are called.

Chorus
You shall be told of our position presently.

Athene
I can know that, if one will give me a clear account.   420

Chorus
We drive from home those who have shed the blood
  of men.

Athene
Where is the place, then, where the killer's flight
  shall end?

Chorus

A place where happiness is nevermore allowed.

Athene

Is he one? Do you blast him to this kind of flight?

Chorus

Yes. He murdered his mother by deliberate choice.   425

Athene

By random force, or was it fear of someone's wrath?

Chorus

Where is the spur to justify man's matricide?

Athene

Here are two sides, and only half the argument.

Chorus

He is unwilling to give or to accept an oath.

Athene

You wish to be called righteous rather than act right.   430

Chorus

No. How so? Out of the riches of your wit, explain.

Athene

I say, wrong must not win by technicalities.

Chorus

Examine him then yourself. Decide it, and be fair.

Athene

You would turn over authority in this case to me?

Chorus

By all means. Your father's degree, and yours, deserve
   as much.   435

Athene

Your turn, stranger. What will you say in answer?
   Speak,

tell me your country and your birth, what has befallen

you, then defend yourself against the anger of these;
if it was confidence in the right that made you sit
to keep this image near my hearth, a supplicant   440
in the tradition of Ixion, sacrosanct.
Give me an answer which is plain to understand.

Orestes
Lady Athene, first I will take the difficult thought
away that lies in these last words you spoke. I am
no supplicant, nor was it because I had a stain   445
upon my hand that I sat at your image. I
will give you a strong proof that what I say is true.
It is the law that the man of the bloody hand must
     speak
no word until, by action of one who can cleanse,
blood from a young victim has washed his blood away.   450
Long since, at the homes of others, I have been
     absolved
thus, both by running waters and by victims slain.

I count this scruple now out of the way. Learn next
with no delay where I am from. I am of Argos
and it is to my honor that you ask the name   455
of my father, Agamemnon, lord of seafarers,
and your companion when you made the Trojan city
of Ilium no city any more. He died
without honor when he came home. It was my mother
of the dark heart, who entangled him in subtle gyves   460
and cut him down. The bath is witness to his death.
I was an exile in the time before this. I came back
and killed the woman who gave me birth. I plead
     guilty.
My father was dear, and this was vengeance for his
     blood.
Apollo shares responsibility for this.   465
He counterspurred my heart and told me of pains
     to come
if I should fail to act against the guilty ones.

This is my case. Decide if it be right or wrong.
I am in your hands. Where my fate falls, I shall
    accept.

Athene
The matter is too big for any mortal man   470
who thinks he can judge it. Even I have not the right
to analyse cases of murder where wrath's edge
is sharp, and all the more since you have come, and
    clung
a clean and innocent supplicant, against my doors.
You bring no harm to my city. I respect your rights.   475
Yet these, too, have their work. We cannot brush
    them aside,
and if this action so runs that they fail to win,
the venom of their resolution will return
to infect the soil, and sicken all my land to death.
Here is dilemma. Whether I let them stay or drive   480
them off, it is a hard course and will hurt. Then, since
the burden of the case is here, and rests on me,
I shall select judges of manslaughter, and swear
them in, establish a court into all time to come.

Litigants, call your witnesses, have ready your proofs 485
as evidence under bond to keep this case secure.
I will pick the finest of my citizens, and come
back. They shall swear to make no judgment that
    is not
just, and make clear where in this action the truth lies.

                                        (*Exit.*)

Chorus
Here is overthrow of all   490
the young laws, if the claim
of this matricide shall stand
good, his crime be sustained.
Should this be, every man will find a way
to act at his own caprice;   495

over and over again in time
to come, parents shall await
the deathstroke at their children's hands.

We are the Angry Ones. But we
shall watch no more over works   500
of men, and so act. We shall
let loose indiscriminate death.
Man shall learn from man's lot, forejudge
the evils of his neighbor's case,
see respite and windfall in storm:
pathetic prophet who consoles   505
with strengthless cures, in vain.

Nevermore let one who feels
the stroke of accident, uplift
his voice and make outcry, thus: 510
"Oh Justice!
Throned powers of the Furies, help!"
Such might be the pitiful cry
of some father, of the stricken
mother, their appeal. Now   515
the House of Justice has collapsed.

There are times when fear is good.
It must keep its watchful place
at the heart's controls. There is
advantage   520
in the wisdom won from pain.
Should the city, should the man
rear a heart that nowhere goes
in fear, how shall such a one
any more respect the right?   525

Refuse the life of anarchy;
refuse the life devoted to
one master.
The in-between has the power
by God's grant always, though   530

166

his ordinances vary.
I will speak in defence
of reason: for the very child
of vanity is violence;
but out of health   535
in the heart issues the beloved
and the longed-for, prosperity.

All for all I say to you:
bow before the altar of right.
You shall not   540
eye advantage, and heel
it over with foot of force.
Vengeance will be upon you.
The all is bigger than you.
Let man see this and take   545
care, to mother and father,
and to the guest
in the gates welcomed, give all rights
that befall their position.

The man who does right, free-willed, without con-
    straint   550
shall not lose happiness
nor be wiped out with all his generation.
But the transgressor, I tell you, the bold man
who brings in confusion of goods unrightly won,
at long last and perforce, when ship toils   555
under tempest must strike his sail
in the wreck of his rigging.

He calls on those who hear not, caught inside
the hard wrestle of water.
The spirit laughs at the hot hearted man,   560
the man who said "never to me," watches him
pinned in distress, unable to run free of the crests.
He had good luck in his life. Now
he smashes it on the reef of Right
and drowns, unwept and forgotten.   565

*(Athene re-enters, guiding twelve citizens chosen
as jurors and attended by a herald.
Other citizens follow.)*

Athene
Herald, make proclamation and hold in the host
assembled. Let the stabbing voice of the Etruscan
trumpet, blown to the full with mortal wind, crash out
its high call to all the assembled populace.
For in the filling of this senatorial ground   570
it is best for all the city to be silent and learn
the measures I have laid down into the rest of time.
So too these litigants, that their case be fairly tried.

(Trumpet call. All take their places. Enter Apollo.)

Chorus
My lord Apollo, rule within your own domain.
What in this matter has to do with you? Declare.   575

Apollo
I come to testify. This man, by observed law,
came to me as suppliant, took his place by hearth
    and hall,
and it was I who cleaned him of the stain of blood.
I have also come to help him win his case. I bear
responsibility for his mother's murder.

(To Athene.)

                                              You   580
who know the rules, initiate the trial. Preside.

Athene (to the Furies)
I declare the trial opened. Yours is the first word.
For it must justly be the pursuer who speaks first
and opens the case, and makes plain what the
    action is.

Chorus
We are many, but we shall cut it short. You, then,   585

168

word against word answer our charges one by one.
Say first, did you kill your mother or did you not?

Orestes
Yes, I killed her. There shall be no denial of that.

Chorus
There are three falls in the match and one has gone
    to us.

Orestes
So you say. But you have not even thrown your man.   590

Chorus
So. Then how did you kill her? You are bound to say.

Orestes
I do. With drawn sword in my hand I cut her throat.

Chorus
By whose persuasion and advice did you do this?

Orestes
By order of this god, here. So he testifies.

Chorus
The Prophet guided you into this matricide?   595

Orestes
Yes. I have never complained of this. I do not now.

Chorus
When sentence seizes you, you will talk a different
    way.

Orestes
I have no fear. My father will aid me from the grave.

Chorus
Kill your mother, then put trust in a corpse! Trust on.

Orestes
Yes. She was dirtied twice over with disgrace.   600

Chorus
Tell me how, and explain it to the judges here.

Orestes
She murdered her husband, and thereby my father too.

Chorus
Of this stain, death has set her free. But you still live.

Orestes
When she lived, why did you not descend and drive
her out?

Chorus
The man she killed was not of blood congenital.　　605

Orestes
But am I then involved with my mother by blood-bond?

Chorus
Murderer, yes. How else could she have nursed you
beneath
her heart? Do you forswear your mother's intimate
blood?

Orestes
Yours to bear witness now, Apollo, and expound
the case for me, if I was right to cut her down.　　610
I will not deny I did this thing, because I did
do it. But was the bloodshed right or not? Decide
and answer. As you answer, I shall state my case.

Apollo
To you, established by Athene in your power,
I shall speak justly. I am a prophet, I shall not　　615
lie. Never, for man, woman, nor city, from my throne
of prophecy have I spoken a word, except
that which Zeus, father of Olympians, might command.
This is justice. Recognize then how great its strength.
I tell you, follow our father's will. For not even　　620
the oath that binds you is more strong than Zeus is
strong.

Chorus

Then Zeus, as you say, authorized the oracle
to this Orestes, stating he could wreak the death
of his father on his mother, and it would have
  no force?

Apollo

It is not the same thing for a man of blood to die   625
honored with the king's staff given by the hand of god,
and that by means of a woman, not with the far cast
of fierce arrows, as an Amazon might have done,
but in a way that you shall hear, o Pallas and you
who sit in state to judge this action by your vote.   630

He had come home from his campaigning. He had
  done
better than worse, in the eyes of a fair judge. She lay
in wait for him. It was the bath. When he was at
its edge, she hooded the robe on him, and in the blind
and complex toils tangled her man, and chopped him
  down.   635

There is the story of the death of a great man,
solemn in all men's sight, lord of the host of ships.
I have called the woman what she was, so that the
  people
whose duty it is to try this case may be inflamed.

Chorus

Zeus, by your story, gives first place to the father's
  death.   640
Yet Zeus himself shackled elder Cronus, his own
father. Is this not contradiction? I testify,
judges, that this is being said in your hearing.

Apollo

You foul animals, from whom the gods turn in disgust,
Zeus could undo shackles, such hurt can be made
  good,   645

171

and there is every kind of way to get out. But once
the dust has drained down all a man's blood, once
  the man
has died, there is no raising of him up again.
This is a thing for which my father never made
curative spells. All other states, without effort   650
of hard breath, he can completely rearrange.

Chorus

See what it means to force acquittal of this man.
He has spilled his mother's blood upon the ground.
  Shall he
then be at home in Argos in his father's house?
What altars of the community shall he use? Is there   655
a brotherhood's lustration that will let him in?

Apollo

I will tell you, and I will answer correctly. Watch.
The mother is no parent of that which is called
her child, but only nurse of the new-planted seed
that grows. The parent is he who mounts. A stranger
  she   660
preserves a stranger's seed, if no god interfere.
I will show you proof of what I have explained.
  There can
be a father without any mother. There she stands,
the living witness, daughter of Olympian Zeus,
she who was never fostered in the dark of the womb   665
yet such a child as no goddess could bring to birth.
In all else, Pallas, as I best may understand,
I shall make great your city and its populace.
So I have brought this man to sit beside the hearth
of your house, to be your true friend for the rest
  of time,   670
so you shall win him, goddess, to fight by your side,
and among men to come this shall stand a strong bond
that his and your own people's children shall be friends.

Athene
Shall I assume that enough has now been said, and tell
the judges to render what they believe a true verdict?   675

Chorus
Every arrow we had has been shot now. We wait
on their decision, to see how the case has gone.

Athene
So then. How shall I act correctly in your eyes?

Apollo
You have heard what you have heard, and as you cast
    your votes,
good friends, respect in your hearts the oath that you
    have sworn.   680

Athene
If it please you, men of Attica, hear my decree
now, on this first case of bloodletting I have judged.
For Aegeus' population, this forevermore
shall be the ground where justices deliberate.
Here is the Hill of Ares, here the Amazons   685
encamped and built their shelters when they came
    in arms
for spite of Theseus, here they piled their rival towers
to rise, new city, and dare his city long ago,
and slew their beasts for Ares. So this rock is named
from then the Hill of Ares. Here the reverence   690
of citizens, their fear and kindred do-no-wrong
shall hold by day and in the blessing of night alike
all while the people do not muddy their own laws
with foul infusions. But if bright water you stain
with mud, you nevermore will find it fit to drink.   695
No anarchy, no rule of a single master. Thus
I advise my citizens to govern and to grace,
and not to cast fear utterly from your city. What
man who fears nothing at all is ever righteous? Such
be your just terrors, and you may deserve and have   700
salvation for your citadel, your land's defence,

such as is nowhere else found among men, neither
among the Scythians, nor the land that Pelops held.
I establish this tribunal. It shall be untouched
by money-making, grave but quick to wrath, watchful   705
to protect those who sleep, a sentry on the land.

These words I have unreeled are for my citizens,
advice into the future. All must stand upright
now, take each man his ballot in his hand, think on
his oath, and make his judgment. For my word is said.   710

Chorus
I give you counsel by no means to disregard
this company. We can be a weight to crush your land.

Apollo
I speak too. I command you to fear, and not
make void the yield of oracles from Zeus and me.

Chorus
You honor bloody actions where you have no right.   715
The oracles you give shall be no longer clean.

Apollo
My father's purposes are twisted then. For he
was appealed to by Ixion, the first murderer.

Chorus
Talk! But for my part, if I do not win the case,
I shall come back to this land and it will feel
    my weight.   720

Apollo
Neither among the elder nor the younger gods
have you consideration. I shall win this suit.

Chorus
Such was your action in the house of Pheres. Then
you beguiled the Fates to let mortals go free from
    death.

Apollo
Is it not right to do well by the man who shows   725
you worship, and above all when he stands in need?

Chorus
You won the ancient goddesses over with wine
and so destroyed the orders of an elder time.

Apollo
You shall not win the issue of this suit, but shall
be made to void your poison to no enemy's hurt.   730

Chorus
Since you, a young god, would ride down my elder age,
I must stay here and listen to how the trial goes,
being yet uncertain to loose my anger on the state.

Athene
It is my task to render final judgment here.
This is a ballot for Orestes I shall cast.   735
There is no mother anywhere who gave me birth,
and, but for marriage, I am always for the male
with all my heart, and strongly on my father's side.
So, in a case where the wife has killed her husband, lord
of the house, her death shall not mean most to me. And if   740
the other votes are even, then Orestes wins.
You of the jurymen who have this duty assigned,
shake out the ballots from the vessels, with all speed.

Orestes
Phoebus Apollo, what will the decision be?

Chorus
Darkness of night, our mother, are you here to watch?   745

Orestes
This is the end for me. The noose, or else the light.

Chorus
Here our destruction, or our high duties confirmed.

175

Apollo
Shake out the votes accurately, Athenian friends.
Be careful as you pick them up. Make no mistake.
In the lapse of judgment great disaster comes.
  The cast 750
of a single ballot has restored a house entire.

Athene
The man before us has escaped the charge of blood.
The ballots are in equal number for each side.

Orestes
Pallas Athene, you have kept my house alive.
When I had lost the land of my fathers you gave me 755
a place to live. Among the Hellenes they shall say:
"A man of Argos lives again in the estates
of his father, all by grace of Pallas Athene, and
Apollo, and with them the all-ordaining god
the Savior"—who remembers my father's death, who
  looked 760
upon my mother's advocates, and rescues me.
I shall go home now, but before I go I swear
to this your country and to this your multitude
of people into all the bigness of time to be,
that never man who holds the helm of my state
  shall come 765
against your country in the ordered strength of spears,
but though I lie then in my grave, I still shall wreak
helpless bad luck and misadventure upon all
who stride across the oath that I have sworn: their
  ways
disconsolate make, their crossings full of evil 770
augury, so they shall be sorry that they moved.
But while they keep the upright way, and hold in high
regard the city of Pallas, and align their spears
to fight beside her, I shall be their gracious spirit.
And so farewell, you and your city's populace. 775
May you outwrestle and overthrow all those who come
against you, to your safety and your spears' success.

(*Exit. Exit also Apollo.*)

Chorus
Gods of the younger generation, you have ridden down
the laws of the elder time, torn them out of my hands.
I, disinherited, suffering, heavy with anger   780
shall let loose on the land
the vindictive poison
dripping deadly out of my heart upon the ground;
this from itself shall breed
cancer, the leafless, the barren   785
to strike, for the right, their low lands
and drag its smear of mortal infection on the ground.
What shall I do? Afflicted
I am mocked by these people.
I have borne what can not   790
be borne. Great the sorrows and the dishonor upon
the sad daughters of night.

Athene
Listen to me. I would not have you be so grieved.
For you have not been beaten. This was the result   795
of a fair ballot which was even. You were not
dishonored, but the luminous evidence of Zeus
was there, and he who spoke the oracle was he
who ordered Orestes so to act and not be hurt.
Do not be angry any longer with this land   800
nor bring the bulk of your hatred down on it, do not
render it barren of fruit, nor spill the dripping rain
of death in fierce and jagged lines to eat the seeds.
In complete honesty I promise you a place
of your own, deep hidden under ground that is yours
  by right   805
where you shall sit on shining chairs beside the hearth
to accept devotions offered by your citizens.

Chorus
Gods of the younger generation, you have ridden down
the laws of the elder time, torn them out of my hands.

I, disinherited, suffering, heavy with anger   810
shall let loose on the land
the vindictive poison
dripping deadly out of my heart upon the ground;
this from itself shall breed
cancer, the leafless, the barren   815
to strike, for the right, their low lands
and drag its smear of mortal infection on the ground.
What shall I do? Afflicted
I am mocked by these people.
I have borne what can not   820
be borne. Great the sorrow and the dishonor upon
the sad daughters of night.

Athene
No, not dishonored. You are goddesses. Do not
in too much anger make this place of mortal men   825
uninhabitable. I have Zeus behind me. Do
we need to speak of that? I am the only god
who knows the keys to where his thunderbolts are
    locked.
We do not need such, do we? Be reasonable
and do not from a reckless mouth cast on the land   830
spells that will ruin every thing which might bear
    fruit.
No. Put to sleep the bitter strength in the black wave
and live with me and share my pride of worship.
    Here
is a big land, and from it you shall win first fruits
in offerings for children and the marriage rite   835
for always. Then you will say my argument was
    good.

Chorus
That they could treat me so!
I, the mind of the past, to be driven under the
    ground
out cast, like dirt!
The wind I breathe is fury and utter hate.   840

Earth, ah, earth
what is this agony that crawls under my ribs?
Night, hear me, o Night,
mother. They have wiped me out   845
and the hard hands of the gods
and their treacheries have taken my old rights away.

Athene
I will bear your angers. You are elder born than I
and in that you are wiser far than I. Yet still
Zeus gave me too intelligence not to be despised.   850
If you go away into some land of foreigners,
I warn you, you will come to love this country. Time
in his forward flood shall ever grow more dignified
for the people of this city. And you, in your place
of eminence beside Erechtheus in his house   855
shall win from female and from male processionals
more than all lands of men beside could ever give.
Only in this place that I haunt do not inflict
your bloody stimulus to twist the inward hearts
of young men, raging in a fury not of wine,   860
nor, as if plucking the heart from fighting cocks,
engraft among my citizens that spirit of war
that turns their battle fury inward on themselves.
No, let our wars range outward hard against the man
who has fallen horribly in love with high renown.   865
No true fighter I call the bird that fights at home.
Such life I offer you, and it is yours to take.
Do good, receive good, and be honored as the good
are honored. Share our country, the beloved of god.

Chorus
That they could treat me so!   870
I, the mind of the past, to be driven under the
    ground
out cast, like dirt!
The wind I breathe is fury and utter hate.
Earth, ah, earth
what is this agony that crawls under my ribs?   875

Night, hear me, o Night,
mother. They have wiped me out
and the hard hands of the gods
and their treacheries have taken my old rights away. 880

Athene
I will not weary of telling you all the good things
I offer, so that you can never say that you,
an elder god, were driven unfriended from the land
by me in my youth, and by my mortal citizens.
But if you hold Persuasion has her sacred place 885
of worship, in the sweet beguilement of my voice,
then you might stay with us. But if you wish to stay
then it would not be justice to inflict your rage
upon this city, your resentment or bad luck
to armies. Yours the baron's portion in this land 890
if you will, in all justice, with full privilege.

Chorus
Lady Athene, what is this place you say is mine?

Athene
A place free of all grief and pain. Take it for yours.

Chorus
If I do take it, shall I have some definite powers?

Athene
No household shall be prosperous without your will. 895

Chorus
You will do this? You will really let me be so strong?

Athene
So we shall straighten the lives of all who worship us.

Chorus
You guarantee such honor for the rest of time?

Athene
I have no need to promise what I can not do.

Chorus

I think you will have your way with me. My hate is
  going.   900

Athene

Stay here, then. You will win the hearts of others,
  too.

Chorus

I will put a spell upon the land. What shall it be?

Athene

Something that has no traffic with evil success.
Let it come out of the ground, out of the sea's water,
and from the high air make the waft of gentle gales   905
wash over the country in full sunlight, and the seed
and stream of the soil's yield and of the grazing
  beasts
be strong and never fail our people as times goes,
the issue of those who worship more your ways, for
  as   910
the gardener works in love, so love I best of all
the unblighted generation of these upright men.
All such is yours for granting. In the speech and
  show
and pride of battle, I myself shall not endure
this city's eclipse in the estimation of mankind.   915

Chorus

I accept this home at Athene's side.
I shall not forget the cause
of this city, which Zeus all powerful and Ares
rule, stronghold of divinities,
glory of Hellene gods, their guarded altar.   920
So with forecast of good
I speak this prayer for them
that the sun's bright magnificence shall break out
  wave
on wave of all the happiness   925
life can give, across their land.

Athene

Here are my actions. In all good will
toward these citizens I establish in power
spirits who are large, difficult to soften.
To them is given the handling entire   930
of men's lives. That man
who has not felt the weight of their hands
takes the strokes of life, knows not whence, not why,
for crimes wreaked in past generations
drag him before these powers. Loud his voice   935
but the silent doom
hates hard, and breaks him to dust.

Chorus

Let there blow no wind that wrecks the trees.
I pronounce words of grace.
Nor blaze of heat blind the blossoms of grown plants,
   nor   940
cross the circles of its right
place. Let no barren deadly sickness creep and kill.
Flocks fatten. Earth be kind
to them, with double fold of fruit   945
in time appointed for its yielding. Secret child
of earth, her hidden wealth, bestow
blessing and surprise of gods.

Athene

Strong guard of our city, hear you these
and what they portend? Fury is a high queen   950
of strength even among the immortal gods
and the undergods, and for humankind
their work is accomplished, absolute, clear:
for some, singing; for some, life dimmed
in tears; theirs the disposition.   955

Chorus

Death of manhood cut down
before its prime I forbid:
girls' grace and glory find

men to live life with them.
Grant, you who have the power.   960
And o, steering spirits of law,
goddesses of destiny,
sisters from my mother, hear;
in all houses implicate,
in all time heavy of hand   965
on whom your just arrest befalls,
august among goddesses, bestow.

Athene
It is my glory to hear how these
generosities
are given my land. I admire the eyes   970
of Persuasion, who guided the speech of my mouth
toward these, when they were reluctant and wild.
Zeus, who guides men's speech in councils, was too
strong; and my ambition
for good wins out in the whole issue.   975

Chorus
This my prayer: Civil War
fattening on men's ruin shall
not thunder in our city. Let
not the dry dust that drinks
the black blood of citizens   980
through passion for revenge
and bloodshed for bloodshed
be given our state to prey upon.
Let them render grace for grace.
Let love be their common will;   985
let them hate with single heart.
Much wrong in the world thereby is healed.

Athene
Are they taking thought to discover that road
where speech goes straight?
In the terror upon the faces of these   990
I see great good for our citizens.

183

While with good will you hold in high honor
these spirits, their will shall be good, as you steer
your city, your land
on an upright course clear through to the end.   995

Chorus
Farewell, farewell. High destiny shall be yours
by right. Farewell, citizens
seated near the throne of Zeus,
beloved by the maiden he loves,
civilized as years go by,   1000
sheltered under Athene's wings,
grand even in her father's sight.

Athene
Goddesses, farewell. Mine to lead, as these
attend us, to where
by the sacred light new chambers are given.   1005
Go then. Sped by majestic sacrifice
from these, plunge beneath the ground. There hold
off what might hurt the land; pour in
the city's advantage, success in the end.
You, children of Cranaus, you who keep   1010
the citadel, guide these guests of the state.
For good things given,
your hearts' desire be for good to return.

Chorus
Farewell and again farewell, words spoken twice
    over,
all who by this citadel,   1015
mortal men, spirits divine,
hold the city of Pallas, grace
this my guestship in your land.
Life will give you no regrets.   1020

Athene
Well said. I assent to all the burden of your prayers,
and by the light of flaring torches now attend
your passage to the deep and subterranean hold,

as by us walk those women whose high privilege
it is to guard my image. Flower of all the land   1025
of Theseus, let them issue now, grave companies,
maidens, wives, elder women, in processional.
In the investiture of purple stained robes
dignify them, and let the torchlight go before
so that the kindly company of these within   1030
our ground may shine in the future of strong men to
   come.

Chorus (by the women who have been forming for
    processional)
Home, home, o high, o aspiring
Daughters of Night, aged children, in blithe proces-
   sional.
Bless them, all here, with silence.   1035

In the primeval dark of earth-hollows
held in high veneration with rights sacrificial
bless them, all people, with silence.

Gracious be, wish what the land wishes,   1040
follow, grave goddesses, flushed in the flamesprung
torchlight gay on your journey.
Singing all follow our footsteps.

There shall be peace forever between these people
of Pallas and their guests. Zeus the all seeing   1045
met with Destiny to confirm it.
Singing all follow our footsteps.

             (*Exeunt omnes, in procession.*)